TRAIN YOUR YOUNG HORSE

with RICHARD MAXWELL

D&C
David and Charles

A DAVID & CHARLES BOOK
Copyright © David & Charles Limited 2008

David & Charles is an F+W Publications Inc. company
4700 East Galbraith Road
Cincinnati, OH 45236

First published in the UK in 2008

Text copyright © Richard Maxwell 2008
Photographs by Matthew Roberts copyright © David & Charles Limited 2008
Except those on page 137 copyright © Mandi Meer and page 139 copyright ©
Susie Gillot

A catalogue record for this book is available from the British Library.

ISBN: 978-0-7153-2799-9 hardback
ISBN: 0-7153-2799-2 hardback

Printed in Singapore by KHL
for David & Charles
Brunel House   Newton Abbot   Devon

Commissioning Editor: Jane Trollope
Editorial Manager: Emily Pitcher
Assistant Editor: Emily Rae
Designer: Jodie Lystor
Production Controller: Beverley Richardson
Photographer: Matthew Roberts

Visit our website at www.davidandcharles.co.uk

David & Charles books are available from all good bookshops; alternatively you can
contact our Orderline on 0870 9908222 or write to us at FREEPOST EX2 110, D&C
Direct, Newton Abbot, TQ12 4ZZ (no stamp required UK only); US customers call
800-289-0963 and Canadian customers call 800-840-5220.

CONTENTS

Introduction

There are several reasons why I felt it was time to rewrite *From Birth to Backing*, my previous best-selling book about bringing on young horses.

The most important reason is that, like every horseman, I'm always learning. Every horse I deal with – and there have been many hundreds since *From Birth to Backing* first appeared – teaches me something, and I'm pleased to say that my techniques have evolved accordingly. It's not that the old ways were wrong, it's just that I've had time to refine them over the years, and I want to share these improvements in a book that people want to read and find easy to follow.

Another reason is that it's not just me who has changed! Over the last ten years, so has the horse industry, and in particular the dynamics of breeding. Once upon a time it was large country estates or stud farms that bred the vast majority of young stock, where a very knowledgeable head lad and his stud grooms were in charge. The mares and foals ran together in large paddocks until weaning. Then at weaning the mares were taken away but the youngsters remained in a group, which is less traumatic for them. I was

at a thoroughbred stud in 2006 where they weaned in this manner and it was good to see how chilled out and relaxed the mares and weanlings were.

However, we now have a large number of young horses being bred by individual owners, quite often in livery yards or small holdings where there isn't the set up to allow 24/7 turnout with another mare and foal. On the livery yard where I currently keep my own horses, there are three mares and their foals but there isn't permanent grazing, so the mares and foals are turned out in the morning and brought in at night. In my eyes what this means is that we now have to think about training our foal at a much earlier age than previously thought acceptable to ensure a safe and pleasant experience for all concerned.

I decided to make use of the internet to get ideas and opinions on what people wanted from another book about training foals and young horses, up to the point of being ridden. It amazed me how many people came up with the same thing, and it was all really basic stuff.

Sometimes I think when we professionals write a book we forget that it's the basics that people need, whether

it's about horsemanship, cooking or anything else. I know that when I first started to cook, I didn't want a book full of gorgeous but complicated recipes; I wanted to be able to boil an egg, put together a simple meal and learn how to get my timing right so that it all came together at the end. So yes, I really did need to be told when to put on the vegetables, and how long they needed to cook for!

Bearing all this in mind, I hope this book will give you a similar range of basic skills, show you how to put them all together and reach a successful conclusion when training your young horse. It is wrong for me or any other horseman to take that knowledge for granted, because anyone who can get the basics right will find anything is possible. You'll soon be flying through the most complicated of recipes and producing perfect results every time!

I have tried to make this book as user-friendly as possible, since it is aimed largely at the amateur horse owner who has decided to buy or breed a youngster. Professionals probably have good systems in place already, but it never does any harm to watch what others are doing and pick up a few more tips and ideas! Finally, I must thank those people who have volunteered their youngsters as models for this book. It would have been impossible to do without them.

The most frequently asked questions that I aim to answer in this book include:

- When do I start to handle my foal?
- How much and how often should I work with a foal?
- When and how do I introduce tack?
- How do I handle barging and bolshiness in a youngster?
- What is the best way to wean to limit emotional stress?
- What kind of work can I do with my youngster before he is ready to ride?

All these areas are covered, although you may not find the questions above answered directly because if you follow the basic principles shown, you shouldn't run into the problems described. Avoiding conflict and stress with knowledgeable handling and careful preparation is by far the best way of giving young horses a confident start in life, and this is the key principle on which I work. For those who do run into problems or have taken on an older horse, I will deal with potential trouble spots throughout the book.

PART 1

Making the decision

Breeding or buying a youngster can be one of the greatest pleasures in life, especially when it all goes to plan. However, life isn't quite like that, but if you follow the guidelines and plans set out in this book, you will definitely be on the right path to a fantastic experience.

This first part is all about the general areas that I think are worth knowing. There aren't any examples of 'how to' but there is lots of valuable information that you should read before you get started. Enjoy your horses and most importantly stay safe. You know your horse better than anyone and if you don't feel that you and your horse are comfortable, move on to something that you both know you can succeed at and come back to the more challenging aspects later.

What's changed and why?

It has been ten years since Jo Sharples and I wrote *From Birth To Backing*. Since then, not only has the colour of my hair changed, but so has the way I work with both horses and people.

I started my career in the army, and when I wrote that first book with Jo, I had only been working with horses outside the military for about three years; this has now become 13 years, and both my knowledge and experience are far more extensive. For example, while researching and laying down the foundations for this book, my wife, Sam, read a comment to me from another book. It advised against the use of dummies on a young horse (yes, this is a stuffed 'pretend person' tied to the saddle instead of a real rider). My response to the statement was, 'Whoever wrote that obviously hasn't had enough experience with horses. Who wrote it?' 'You did', she replied.

At that time, I had only come into contact with horses that had been traumatized and needed re-backing as a result of a dummy being used wrongly. I had certainly never used a dummy myself but that changed when I had a particularly difficult horse in to back and I decided to try a dummy in this instance. I discovered that when used at the right time on the right horse, the result was highly successful. So wider experience has lead to a change in some of my opinions.

Using a dummy

Discovering groundwork

In those early days my main tools for starting and training youngsters were join-up and long-lining. This was what I knew and I always did the job to the best of my ability, but the more horses I worked with, the more I began to look at matters differently. Slowly but surely, as a horseman I started to change. I have always considered myself a forward-thinking horseman, and learning new things has always excited me. Now when I back a youngster from a very early age, I have a much more extensive groundwork toolkit at my disposal, from rope work to all the desensitization exercises. I go through a mental checklist, and until each section is perfect, I don't move on to the next. This gives me a better opportunity to produce a really nice, well-behaved young horse. Working in more depth means I don't leave anything to chance, whether it's preparing for the saddle, bridle, clippers or loading.

Another huge 'light bulb' moment with young horses was realizing the importance of repetition. It's no good getting something right once or twice, it has to be right a lot, and preferably every time if the horse is to learn correctly. This topic is covered later in the book and will show you how and why repetition is so important.

I strongly believe that horses with loading problems have taught me the most. This is mainly because I spend so much time in front of them, watching their facial expressions, that I can almost see how they think and what they are going to do next. I always school horses with loading problems before going to the trailer so that they understand the principles of pressure and release. I also ensure the horse knows that I can move him around and have control of all directions – forward, backwards and side to side – while using a rope and halter.

Whilst working a horse like this for a client, she told me I was very similar to a trainer called Pat Parelli. At that time I hadn't heard much about Pat Parelli, so I did some research and went to see his next UK demonstration.

Until then I hadn't thought of using groundwork in areas other than loading or starting stall problems in racehorses, so Pat's demo was a huge learning experience for me. Fortunately I'm a visual learner and where horses are concerned I only have to see something once or twice for it to make sense. Other ideas I would credit to Pat's demo were the importance of controlling the horse's feet and the science behind why horses become calmer when asked to think (see pages 36–39).

Over the next few years I developed my groundwork and formulated my own system. The number of horses I failed with reduced greatly. I'm not saying that I didn't have the occasional horse that I felt I had failed with, but I think of failure as part of the learning curve and every horse I have not succeeded with has taught me something to take on to the next. A great horseman once said to me that if you say that you've never failed with a horse, then you are either lying or you haven't done enough horses. I would definitely agree.

Extensive preparation

ROUND PENS AND JOIN-UP

When so-called natural horsemanship techniques started to become well-known in the UK, it was (and still is) very common to see a metal round pen as a key tool of the trade. I used to have one myself, but I no longer use it. This is not because I don't believe in them, but simply because the average horse owner doesn't have one. The most important rule of horsemanship I have learnt is that whoever has control of the horse's feet (i.e. their movement and direction) has total control. By this, I don't mean that you have to be a control freak, but you do have to be in control of the situation and this rule has to apply in all situations, regardless of your horse's age.

Join-up is just about controlling movement and direction, which I can do without a round pen. I use a halter and rope to connect with the horse instead, and no longer need to chase a horse around to achieve respect and join-up.

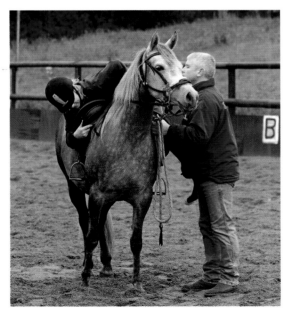
Working without a round pen

Owner involvement

The debate about whether or not to use a round pen brings me onto the most important way in which I have changed how I work. I now demand a far greater level of involvement from the horse's owner, because I know that is the route to solving the horse's problems permanently rather than just when I am on the scene!

In the early days I was really happy to work with just the horse, either through the backing process or their problems afterwards. The owner would come to visit at the weekend, I would show them my stuff then at the end of their horse's stay they would ride their horse and go home. I never really gave it much thought; by nature I am a shy person and the less I had to speak the better.

But I went through a stage of the occasional horse going home and within six weeks the owner would call to say things had all gone back to square one or they were having a few issues. I just didn't understand what was going wrong, as most of the time I'd found the horse perfectly straightforward to deal with.

By chance, I found my answer when we had a case of strangles on the yard. Nothing could come in or out but we still had bills to pay. So I started to go out to owners at their own homes and show them the tools they needed to start sorting out their own problems. BINGO! That's where I had been going wrong! I was only looking after the horse in the relationship, but this was only half the problem – I should also have been dealing with owners and the horse–owner relationship. Overnight the phone calls saying it was going backwards grew less and less. I had to overcome my shyness but it's been worth it and as a horseman I progressed to another level.

Groundwork has really changed the dynamic of how I work with horses

Making a plan

The pyramid that I talked about in *Maximize Your Horsemanship* plays a large part in everything that I do. It's having a plan that helps me and also my clients to achieve their goals.

The pyramid format is not a new idea in horsemanship, but each one must be adapted for each purpose, so the pyramid for training a young horse is different to other training pyramids although the principles are the same. Having solid foundations and a broad base of support is the most important part of any training. My pyramids are in my head, I don't need to write them down, but if it helps you to remember and to put everything into an order, then write one out and stick it on the tack room wall (see page 12). I will share my checklist with you as we go, and it will become clear why it is so important to follow a logical progression and tick each box before moving on to the next stage. By doing this you will succeed at every level in producing a lovely youngster for life.

Anyone who has read my previous books will find a degree of repetition here, but I believe this is necessary in order to refresh your memories and give the background to those who are starting from scratch. Reminding people of the process is essential and cannot be left out. However, there is plenty that is new to everyone.

Enjoy your horses, stay safe and only do things when you feel ready and are confident of a successful outcome.

I do not desensitize horses to turn them into automatons but to make them safer to be around

The training pyramid

A training pyramid is a useful tool in establishing firm foundations with your youngster that you can build upon. Following an organized training regime with a logical progression will help you and your horse achieve your goals.

SAFE, NICE YOUN
HORSE

BACKING (PAGES 130–131)

RIDING AWAY
(PAGE 132)

CIRCLING WORK AND
INTRODUCING
THE TACK (PAGES 100–101
AND 118–121)

LONG-LINING, TRANSITIONS,
LEFT AND RIGHT AND
MOUTHING (PAGES 124–127
AND 122–123)

INTRODUCIN
NEW SITUATIO
E.G. LOADING IN
TRAILERS (PAGE
92–107)

IMPRINTING (PAGES 52-3)

EARLY HALTER WORK, TYING
UP, HANDLING FEET AND
VULNERABLE AREAS (PAGES
54–61, 64–65 AND 80–81)

TRUSTING AND
RESPECTING
YOU IN ALL
SITUATIONS

EARLY DESENSITIZATION:
WALKING OVER, THROUGH
AND UNDER THINGS
(PAGES 82–89)

FURTHER RIDDEN
EDUCATION AND
HACKING OUT
(PAGES 133–135)

LEADING FROM
ANOTHER HORSE AND
INTRODUCING TACK
(PAGES 108–109)

PREPARING FOR A RIDER,
DUMMY IF NECESSARY
(PAGES 128–129)

EARLY GROUNDWORK
(PAGES 62–63)

USING LEFT BRAIN MORE
THAN RIGHT BRAIN
(PAGES 36–39)

PREPARING FOR WEANING,
LEADING INDEPENDENTLY
FROM MUM
(PAGES 66–67)

Taking on a youngster

When you take on a youngster, be in no doubt that you are taking on a huge responsibility. Your horse's education, and his future quality of life, will be entirely down to you. Don't be fooled either by the old theory that a baby is a 'blank canvas' and therefore trouble-free. Like every animal, horses start to learn from the moment they are born, so even a weanling will already have had at least six months education (or mis-education!) before you get him.

I believe that these first six months of a horse's education are probably the most important, and if you are responsible for breeding a foal, then you are also responsible for shaping that foal's life and training him to be the kind of horse that everyone wants around.

As I mentioned in the introduction, the dynamics of breeding have changed – now it is taking place on livery yards and small holdings rather than on large stud farms. I think this is why pre-weaning training is so important. Foals are being handled far more than they would have been in the past, when they might have been left to run (and learn manners) in a herd situation. This means that all their behavioural influences come from a human source, which is why it is so important for the human in their lives to set a good example. This does not necessarily mean being the most loving owner in the world, but being the best leader you possibly can be, since that is what actually matters most to the horse.

Tough love

For a successful future together, you need to honestly assess your own strengths and weaknesses as well as those of the horse. I've noted that what takes many owners outside their comfort zone is the need to be a leader to their animals, rather than a friend or mother. It is difficult not to do what comes naturally to you as a human, nurturing foals in a sentimental way as if they were a human baby, especially since they are so cute! However, you are doing the foal no favours treating it as a baby; mares are quite tough on their foals, adopting a strict but fair approach, this is for the foal's own protection being a flight animal.

Tough love is always much harder on the owners than it is on the foal. Your foal won't be feeling as uncomfortable about it as you are so don't let those human emotions get in the way of a successful relationship.

Another area where amateur breeders often struggle is remaining calm when things go wrong or the horse has a mad, unpredictable moment – as all youngsters do from time to time. If you react to their behaviour, you will make them feel insecure and unsure. You must be a stable and consistent person whenever you are around youngsters.

ARE YOU READY TO OWN A YOUNGSTER?

Before you decide to either put your mare in foal or buy a weanling, ask yourself the following questions:

• Have I got the knowledge and the facilities to be able to breed a youngster successfully, and if not, am I prepared to do my homework and create a workable solution?
• Why am I breeding a foal? And what is his role in life going to be?
• Can I be an assertive leader and get mentally tough if I need to? Foals are just like children and they will try your patience, jump on your head and totally overreact to simple requests.
• Can I be fair and consistent in my training – no sentimental huggy-kissy stuff with no rules one day, while expecting respect the next?
• Have I got the patience to explain clearly what I require to the horse, and the understanding that although I have chosen to use a more natural approach, there is still nothing natural about what I am asking of the horse?
• Am I in a position financially to see a young horse through good times and bad? For example, it's not at all unusual for young horses to get themselves in trouble and require extensive veterinary treatment.

If you decide to take on a youngster you must be prepared to assert your leadership, when necessary, in order to gain the foal's respect. He must learn early on that certain behaviour is unacceptable

MAX: MY EXPERIENCES AS A BREEDER

Despite the highs and lows, there is nothing more rewarding than breeding and training your own foal. I was like a proud clucky father with the two I bred, and when our training sessions went well and they started to progress through each level, I felt as proud as I did when my sons spoke for the first time or rode their bikes without stabilizers!

The real icing on the cake is when they start to come into contact with people such as farriers, vets, dentists and judges and they are polite and well-mannered whilst still maintaining their character. There's nothing like a compliment about good manners – not dissimilar to a good parents' evening!

Fly was the first horse we bred, and we thought long and hard about what we wanted out of the whole affair. I wanted two things. The first was to see if I bred a horse and implemented everything I had learned, how easy that horse would be to train. My belief was that with the correct start any horse could maintain character and personality but have a trainable mind. The second was to see, if I looked into it enough, whether I could breed a horse for a specific job, bearing in mind that I had no experience of breeding.

My mare was called Patsy O'Reilly and was a failed hurdler by Callernish, sire of Imperial Call, a Cheltenham Gold Cup winner. Her owners sent her to me with some issues when I first started taking in horses. She was so tenacious that the first thing she tried to do was jump out of the round pen. She was *very* dominant and did not like me pushing her around. This was the first time I had encountered this sort of mare, and I loved that she challenged me every step of the way and made me think outside the box. She was a horse that taught me a lot.

Some years later, her owners called to say she was for sale and Sam, knowing I really liked her, bought her for my birthday (I know, lucky boy!). We show jumped and evented but eventually I had to retire her as an injury she suffered when younger returned and it became too much for her to work in an outline. Time to have a foal I thought.

She had amazing ability but I needed to put her to a stallion that would give her more bone, as she was very fine. I also needed a calming influence to counteract her hotness and, finally, I wanted to breed an event horse, as that really was my passion at that time. I eventually selected Welton Crackerjack as he had everything I wanted in a sire.

Patsy gave birth to a fabulous colt foal in 1999 and we named him Fly after my favourite horse in the Household Cavalry, Fly By Night the IV. Unfortunately, when he was four, circumstances dictated that we had to sell him. He went to Ellie Hughes, a young event rider who has done amazingly well with him. She named him Spread the Word and in the spring of 2007 he went Advanced. One of the things Ellie said to me in the early years of owning him was how amazing it was to own a horse that was so trainable and yet maintained all his character. She told me that as a four year old he would lead the older event horses out on a hack as nothing phased him.

That comment made it all worthwhile and I knew that I had a winning formula in terms of training and backing young horses regardless of their job in life. A safe hack is a valuable hack.

Ellie Hughes with Spread the Word (Fly)

10 principles for youngsters

Like every well-run school, you will need a training plan or 'curriculum' of varied and appropriate lessons to teach your horse, week by week. The specific tasks you should include are covered in Part 3, but there are also some general training principles that should apply to all your dealings with your horse no matter what the stage of training. I find these help me to stay on track, but the principles for youngsters are slightly different from those found in *Maximize Your Horsemanship,* and are not listed in order of importance. For me they are all crucial.

1. Time

Time is the most crucial tool in training young horses as everything takes that much longer to sink in. If you try to rush matters, you won't truly have succeeded in laying strong foundations, and everything you go on to do will be superficial.

Be fair to yourself too. When attempting something new, don't choose a day where you have had a bad time at work, have got the shopping to do, are taking the kids to a party and are going out for dinner that night. Your patience and energy will not be up to it!

While on the subject of time, I also believe strongly in allowing horses 'thinking time' to enable them to process what has just happened, and it should always follow a period of pressure. Thinking time with young horses is even more important.

It is so tempting to rush things when working with a youngster. However, allowing him a few moments of thinking time generally lets him work out what you want by himself. Here you can see Manny figuring out that all I want is for him to release the pressure by turning and facing me

2. Planning and preparation

Make a plan of your training programme so that it is in a logical order and makes sense. This will ensure that you cover all the tasks needed to help your foal to become a nice trainable youngster. On a smaller scale, you need a rough plan for the days you are going to spend working with your foal so time isn't wasted. Have everything ready, even if that means roping someone else in to help, and make sure they have allowed a generous amount of time, not just a half hour before they have to dash off because this is tempting fate with a young horse!

Having someone to help in the early stages means you can make the best use of the small amounts of time you have with your foal

When you are going to introduce something new to your horse, such as a hose, make sure you have everything set out before you tackle the situation. For more on bathing see pages 94–95

3. Understanding the value of pressure (your horse already does)

Foals understand the value of pressure from the minute their mum starts to interact with them, so if you start to work your youngster soon after he is born, everything will make complete sense to him.

Pressure is a marker that we use so that foals understand the difference between right and wrong, which is exactly what mum will do. There is often a misconception about pressure, this is probably because we try to humanize it; to us pressure equals stress, whereas when used in the correct way the horse will perceive pressure as a normal way of communicating. Pressure is only unfair when it is excessive, when it is forcing your foal to do something he cannot comfortably achieve either physically or mentally.

When a horse uses pressure to discipline another horse, he is always very quick to remove that pressure, and you must remember this. Your youngster will respect you far more if you take off the pressure quickly once the right answer has been given. In the early days the pressure you apply will be very obvious, but as your horse responds, the pressure can become less and less until it is almost invisible.

Horses use pressure and release all the time when they are with each other. It took Manny here seconds to move away from the pressure of the halter and come towards me. We tend to train older horses away from what comes naturally

4. Reward the 'try' not the result – praise every positive action no matter how small

Even for humans, praise is a highly motivating training tool, but it is even more so for the horse. After all, they aren't interested in salary rises or promotions, so what else is in it for them? Continual praise for a job well done is worth huge amounts. I have a dyslexic son, and every word he reads is the equivalent of us trying to climb Mount Everest. If he had to wait until he had read a whole book before being told he had done well, he would give up, so what we have to do is quietly praise him every few words. Hearing words such as 'excellent', 'well done', 'you're doing brilliantly' makes a huge difference, then he can't wait to read the next page.

The same should be done when training horses. If a horse is worried by something, watch his body and his face, as it will tell you loads about what he is thinking (see 'Reading your horse', pages 32–35). Even a sway in the right direction means that he is starting to think in the right way. Release any pressure you may have for a split second to acknowledge the try, which is the equivalent of saying 'good job, well done' under your breath. However, do NOT over praise as it will lose its value.

When you can see your horse is trying and making the right forward-thinking movements, reward him by removing the pressure. He will quickly work out that to come off the pressure is so much easier than fighting it. Here I was looking for this youngster to move his off hind leg forward. As he was doing as I asked, I momentarily put slack in rope – rewarding the try

5. Firm but fair

Teaching people to be firm enough without resorting to aggression is one of the hardest things to do, but getting the balance right is imperative when working with youngsters so you must get your head around doing just that. When training your horse, it takes an equal measure of firmness and fairness to be successful, and one doesn't work without the other. Getting it right is the key to gaining your horse's respect.

Here Wonky decides that he would rather run over the top of me, but quietly and firmly I let him know that his behaviour is not acceptable

Now I continue with the task in hand and Wonky is doing really well. I didn't dwell on his mistake and he didn't hold his discipline against me. Remember you are entitled to defend yourself

6. Be clear in what you ask

There is nothing more frustrating than being asked to do something that you don't understand, whether this is because the question wasn't worded correctly or because you haven't a clue what the questioner is on about.

Problems frequently arise with horses because of confusion, which can cause a horse to become agitated and this is when communication can break down. Often the request is then made more harshly but not more clearly and the handler will perceive their horse to be ignorant when in fact he just doesn't understand.

Being too subtle in your ask in the early stages of training is being UNCLEAR. Here I am using the rope in large overarm sweeping movements so that this youngster is very clear about me wanting him to move away. I will eventually only have to use my hand to get the same response

7. Say what you mean and mean what you say

This is such a good statement and probably one of the hardest to carry out. It's all about being consistent. If you want your horse to stand and you ask him to but then he wanders around and you allow that behaviour, then you are not meaning what you say. Just like people, horses will latch onto that fact and will start to dominate the relationship. Even if getting them to stand takes half an hour or longer, it doesn't matter, they will quickly understand that you mean what you say and eventually when you ask them to stand, they will do it on the first ask.

It took several attempts to get Clemmie to stand in her own space. When she crept forward I would put her back on her spot. I repeated this pattern until she was happy to stand in her own space

8. Don't start something you can't finish

This is especially true with foals and youngsters. As they are at the most important stage of their life in terms of learning, you will quickly teach them who is in control of a situation – whether it is you or them. A foal, even at that young age, is much quicker and stronger than any human, so it is imperative that they learn that they are not top of the pecking order. Go back to your plan and organize yourself so that you set up a win-win situation and not a lose-lose one.

Sometimes sticking with a task can be the most difficult thing to do, but if you give up on something half way through, your horse will know that you don't mean what you say and the next time will be even harder

This session probably took 20 minutes and after about 15 minutes it's so tempting to give up and think you won't achieve your goal. Stick with it, you'll get there in the end and the next day will be easier. If you spend 20 minutes and then give up, the next day you will be at it for 30 minutes and so on

9. Make the right thing easy

From the horse's point of view, there has to be a benefit in getting it right. I use pressure and release as a concept in training, because this takes what horses understand naturally and uses it in our everyday dealings with them. When your youngster gets it right, there has to be a period of no pressure and no nagging as a reward.

When you are asking your horse to do something that worries him, it is important that he knows the difference between the right and wrong response. In this first picture, I have put Wonky under pressure. He doesn't want to go near the tarp, but as soon as he gets it right, I take all the pressure off until he makes a mistake. It only takes another moment for him to step on the tarp

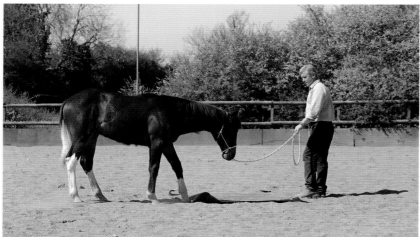

10. Don't 'baby' your baby

Remember the principles of tough love. Try not to let your youngster become over-familiar, and don't make excuses for unacceptable behaviour just because he is young. They grow up fast and even at an early stage, they are cleverer and stronger than you think!

When your youngster has a moment because he is worried or confused, it is hard not to stop and give him a rub to reassure him, but all this does is confirm to him that he was right to have a moment. Quietly persist and as soon as you get the required behaviour, you can give him a rub and then ask the question again.

The importance of repetition

This is a training principle that deserves a mention in its own right, because repetition has become a such an essential tool in the process that I use. It has become apparent to me over the years that, as a rule, we don't put a high enough value on getting things right the first time, and then repeating them again and again. When things go well, we become complacent and think the horse has learned the correct behavioural response, which isn't necessarily true; when things go badly, we keep repeating unwanted behaviour, which can only make a problem more deep rooted.

CASE HISTORY

I recently went out to see a grand prix dressage rider because her horse wasn't coping in a show environment. We went through some training processes, but the rider just wasn't getting the message, and kept telling me what her trainer had said she should do. Eventually, I asked her when was she going to accept that whatever her trainer had told her obviously wasn't working, or else she wouldn't have had to call me! Clearly the processes she had been shown weren't effective on her horse and at what point was she going to accept that and to change her course of action? All she was doing was proving to the horse that she wasn't in control and his reaction (to disobey her) was the right one because it always worked.

REPETITION, REPETITION, REPETITION

The importance of good and correct repetition shows particularly well with loading problems. One of the first loading problems I ever went out to took me seven hours – *seven hours*! I tell you, when that horse finally loaded I burst into tears! It was one of the hardest things I have ever done. Anyway, I popped the horse on and off the lorry a few times and went home. I can't tell you how depressed I felt when I got a call a week later to say that the horse had refused to load again, my heart sank to the bottom of my boots.

On my return visit I loaded that horse probably a good 60–70 times, and then instructed the owners to repeat this amount of loads for the next ten days. What this gave me at the end of the ten days was a horse that had loaded without hesitation about 600 times, which is probably more times than the average horse is loaded in a life time.

It doesn't matter what you are introducing for the first time, remember the amount of positive repetitions is important. Here I am working with a plastic bag folded up small and patting Wonky all over until I get a positive reaction. Here he has started to relax. Notice that he is about to lick and chew. I can now think about opening the bag

A question of numbers

Repetition works because the horse forgets what it was like to get it wrong. Physically and mentally, they are geared to doing things right and it eventually doesn't enter their head not to do it, unless of course they are given a fright.

I call this my numbers game, and when I am trying to change a pattern of established behaviour or introduce new stimuli that will cause a horse to react, I think of how many times the average pleasure horse will be asked to do the task in hand over a year and aim to repeat that over period of five to seven days.

For example, when I am introducing the saddle for the first time I will allow the horse to express himself with the saddle, then once he has got that out of his system, I will take the saddle off and put it straight back on again and ask him to go off in a different direction. Once he has got used to that, I will repeat it so that by the end of the first day that horse has had the saddle on and off its back at least 50 times. I would then repeat that for the next five to seven days, so in total that horse will have had a saddle put on and taken off his back over 250 times, which is more than the average pleasure horse has in a year. Even a youngster will develop a complete acceptance of the saddle by then. We need to apply this to all aspects of our horsemanship if we are trying to change something or teach something new.

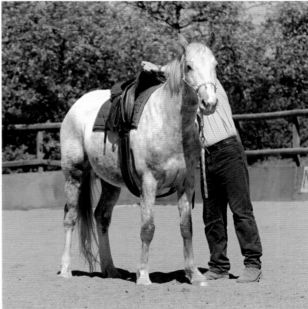

Introducing the first saddle is important but even more so is repeating the process successfully a lot of times. Here you see Hermione with her first saddle. When she stops, I bring her back and repeat the process. I am looking for perfect repetitions – if I were to have a bad one I would add another one on

RULES AND REASONS FOR REPETITION

It is no good doing more of the same stuff if it isn't working. When trying to change a horse's behaviour you need to:

1. First decide that you are absolutely committed to changing this unwanted behaviour.

2. Ask yourself how you are going to do it and then set aside a block of time when you are going to work on it.

3. When you get it right, don't think 'let's end on a good note', because the next day you will be almost back at square one. Repeat it at least ten times and repeat the next day and the next until it's almost second nature.

4. Don't be grateful for small things. This is no time for compromise. Go for the end result and don't accept anything less. Praise the horse's efforts when he tries, but don't settle for that. He actually needs to get it right and to see things through to a conclusion in order to learn and in order for you to really be able to reward him.

Redirection and perception

Repetition when training horses is useful in two important areas: first, to redirect something that has gone wrong and change the horse's habitual patterns of behaviour (e.g. a horse that will never load quickly and easily, if at all); and second, to change the horse's perception of a situation (e.g. the horse doesn't load quickly and easily because he has found previous exeriences of the same situation stressful and uncomfortable).

A horse's perception of something is usually worse than the reality. To change that we need to show him that there's no need to be frightened or panicked, we can't do this by getting it 'a little bit' right. It has to be completely right, lots of times.

Wonky's owner has already told me that he doesn't like his head, neck and ears to be touched. I work with Wonky by repeatedly putting my hand between his ears until we get a positive response and then continue until Wonky is completely relaxed

Reading your horse

Establishing a clear means of communication between you and your horse is essential if the two of you are ever going to learn from each other (and yes, the horse will teach you as much as you teach him if you are prepared to listen!).

When you are working around your horse and introducing new tasks, it is worth paying attention to the aspects of his body language that indicate how he is feeling about things. This will help you to exercise good judgement and also to predict how the horse might react, so that you will know how to handle the situation in the best way to achieve a successful outcome.

There are no hard and fast rules when it comes to equine body language; indeed, some people say that none of it is proven. Yet I work with thousands of horses and when they all behave in a similar way when confronted with the same situations, I feel that there has to be a link there. It certainly does no harm to be aware of it, and I do feel quite strongly that some of the experts that dispute the value of understanding body language haven't worked with the vast number of horses that horsemen like myself have.

When I first started to work with horses using join-up, I was always told not to look horses in the eye. But now I feel that you must look them in the eye so that you can read what they are going to do – the difference is how you look at them. Don't stare aggressively, just glance and observe from a distance. This has really helped me predict equine behaviour, whether it is scientifically proven or not. For example, during a loading problem if the horse looks left and then right, I know it is highly likely that he is going to rear next. In my experience, horses invariably display the same patterns of behaviour.

Head position

Look at the following pictures and you will see that when I first introduce something new, the horse's head will go up and he will be ready for flight. This indicates initial anxiety about what you are asking, but by quiet repetition he will start to lower his head. This is when you will know that he is starting to feel more comfortable and understand what you are asking.

If you have a horse that naps or is spooky when ridden, he will actually give you quite a lot of notice as his head will come up as an early warning signal. This is the moment to put into place the tools you have in your box to avoid unwanted behaviour.

Nose

In young horses, particularly those under one year old, I find that their noses (specifically the nostril area and upper lip) is a sure sign of whether they are happy or worried. When you introduce something new, they will 'beak' their nose, and it will become quite pointed and protrude over their bottom lip (see the photo, right). As they begin to feel more comfortable, their nose will relax. After this period of worry, they will also begin to lick and chew.

Licking and chewing

This happens when a horse is thinking and processing information. When you introduce something new, you will know when the horse is starting to digest the information because he will begin licking and chewing (see photo below). This indicates to me that he understands and I can repeat the question. After licking and chewing, horses normally sigh.

Sighing

When people emerge from a period of intense pressure, a big sigh is in order and horses are just the same. When you ask them to do something they are unsure of, they will hold their breath, and when they get the message, they lick and chew, and then sigh. At that point all is OK with the world. Listen out for it, it is a good sign.

Gulping

If you are introducing something to your horse that involves high visual and tactile pressure, to which he would normally respond with the flight reflex but is unable to do so because of the environment or equipment you are using, he will generally gulp with relief when he comes out the other side. It is very audible. When you do a lot of desensitization work with horses (see pages 82–89), you will hear them gulp a lot. Once they have gulped, praise them, as they really have to work hard through the fear and need reassurance.

Eyes

Even if you don't believe that eyes are the window to the soul, the shape of a horse's eye does say a lot about how he feels about a given situation.

If you have that 'gobstopper' look where the eye is large, round and very rarely blinks (in some instances you can almost hear the eyelid snap shut), this means your horse is truly wary and worried about a situation or what you are asking (see photo above). It is important to work through this quietly and calmly until the eye changes to an almond shape and the blinking becomes more normal. The horse's head will generally be up when this is happening; if your horse's head is low and he is blinking normally, this means he is OK with everything (see photo above right).

Yawning

If your horse starts to yawn while working (I don't mean when they are standing with their head over the stable door!) he is emotionally drained. With a young horse, the batteries are truly flat and they will not learn anything further, so try to end a session before you get to the yawn stage. With foals it can happen quite quickly, so keep sessions short.

A horse that yawns has been using the left side of his brain (the side of reason), so it is not a bad thing; a horse working with the right side of the brain (instinctive and reactive) cannot yawn at the same time.

Poking the dock

This generally happens when horses are apprehensive while on the move. For example, when you first introduce the saddle, you will probably notice that the bottom of the dock will poke through their tail. This means that they are unsure about the situation, but as they become more comfortable, their dock will assume the normal position. Work through the situation quietly and calmly until you have a relaxed, swinging tail.

Tripod stance

This is when your youngster puts his front feet together and spreads his back legs, giving the visual impression of a tripod. This is a 'No way. Can't. Shan't. Won't!' moment where he refuses to go forward.

Foals often do this early on in their handling when you are trying to halter train and lead. The other times I see this is during loading problems and in ridden nappy horses.

Never make this situation a test of strength because you will lose and could hurt your horse. You must make the horse move and uproot his balance one way or another. If you are on the ground, take up the rope and move towards his quarters to turn the head off its central axis. If you are riding, you can do the same. This is why it is so important to have these moves in place on the ground as the horse gets older.

Pet lip

By this I don't mean horses that stand in their stable with a droopy bottom lip.

Over the years that I have been working with horses I started to notice that a small percentage dropped their lower lip when I was putting some form of pressure on them, particularly in loading problems. Straight after dropping their lip they would have a temper tantrum and explode.

When I find myself presented with this pet lip, I know to expect an explosive reaction and prepare myself – I do NOT put any more pressure on them, I make sure that I am stood away from the front feet as the explosion generally involves the feet.

These horses are quite difficult to work with and everything takes a bit longer, but to change the behaviour pattern you must quietly stick to your task or you will always be quietly controlled by them.

Left and right brain thinking

Most mammals have two functionally distinctive brain hemispheres. The left brain hemisphere is the logically cognitive, interactive, analytical and communicative centre – it is the thinking part of the brain; the right brain is the centre of emotion, feeling and reactivity.

As people we generally use both sides of our brain depending on the situation; we are able to use logical reasoning quite easily. Horses, however, have survived by relying heavily on their right brain where they have most of their instinctive and emotional responses, so anger, fear, confusion are all part of their right-brain thinking. The hard wiring of the horse is to automatically react and respond to danger without hesitation.

It is crucial to know how the horse's brain works when put under the pressure of being trained or retrained. All the things we do with our domesticated horses ask them to overrule their natural instincts, but we need to do it in such a way that we don't take away all their personality that makes them the horses we love.

Most horses work emotionally just below the point of being out of control. Being designed not to think but to respond to his environment and to react accordingly (i.e. engage the right brain), requires the horse to use adrenaline to fuel his natural inclination to block out logical thinking and run with his instincts.

Through domestication and training we are trying to change this process so that the horse will use the left side of his brain (i.e. the analytical, thinking side) because in doing so, he releases endorphins that block out the use of adrenaline, resulting in a calming affect. Once a horse gets used to doing this he will become much happier in his training, more co-operative and easier to train. It also means you have a safer horse in unexpected situations.

Clemmie struggled to work on a circle when we first started. Now that she is using the left side of her brain, she has become calm and is able to learn

Once your youngster is working using the left side of his brain, you will be able to present him with new challenges confidently

Some right-brain management concepts

As owner and/or rider you must establish yourself as the leader in the horse's mind; this is where your basic ground training skills will come into play. Remember that a frightened horse is unable to learn, so no matter what reaction you get from your horse, you must remain calm and passive until he has worked out that everything is safe. A horse can be taught to work through a situation and to follow the cues and aids of the rider/owner in unfamiliar and threatening situations. This is especially so when you are riding your horse in a situation where there is the potential for him to be worried. If you have him well trained to listen to you and to use the left side of his brain, he is less likely to be dangerous. He is entitled to some spookiness but should not be so worried that he takes control of the situation.

The more you ask your horse to use the left side of his brain, the more successful he will become, and his confidence will grow, which will result in him using the right side of his brain less and less.

There will be points in your training where your horse will go slightly 'right brained', but I look at this as a stress release, not unlike us. I know I have days where I need to go for a run to get rid of pent up energy, or even aggression. My wife, Sam, occasionally uses a punch bag (in the gym of course) if she needs to get rid of any aggression. It's completely normal.

We have to accept that training is going to generate some stress and that the horse will reach a point where he has to relieve it. This doesn't mean we will expect the horse to always respond unfavourably to stress, but that we don't let it upset us and we work methodically to bring it under control.

Most successful trainers of difficult horses have a few things in common: they establish their leadership position, gain the horse's confidence, and set up some kind of training regimen where the horse ultimately has to mentally process the situation and deal with it other than through flight.

Emptying the stress tank

A prey animal has to flee from danger. Therefore when he sees, hears or smells something disconcerting, it generates stress. If the stressful stimulation continues or intensifies, the stress builds up until it reaches a point where he either takes flight or fights. This flight or fight response will continue until the stress is relieved and the horse returns to a tranquil state. This is critical if the horse is to survive among predators.

One can think of the horse as having a 'stress tank' inside his right brain. Each horse has an individual rate at which he fills his tank. Each horse also has a means to naturally drain the tank. A horse that fills quickly and drains slowly might be described as hot or volatile, while a horse that fills slowly and empties readily may be considered cold or laid back. How a horse handles his stress tank is a product of his genetics as well as his life's experiences.

While we can't change a horse's genetic predisposition, we can affect his life's experiences so that he is less prone to fill his stress tank and is more efficient at keeping it drained. When stress management is included in the training process (in the context of teaching the horse how to manage his stress), then the handler will usually see significant improvements in the horse's behaviour.

This youngster is worried about having his feet picked up – which as a flight animal is a normal reaction. However, as a domesticated animal, he needs to have his feet handled. By using groundwork and sticking to the task he learns to control his fear so that I am able to handle his feet by the end of the session

Using the walk

When a horse is in 'self-preservation' mode, he is operating primarily on his right brain hemisphere ('flight or fight' instinct) and can't learn much. If we can stimulate his curiosity during a training session, he will use his left brain hemisphere, which is his thinking and learning apparatus. Fortunately for us, horses don't efficiently use both hemispheres at the same time, instead they flip from one mode to another, so if we can keep his thinking side active, he'll be less likely to panic or become violent.

With this in mind think about our main three paces: walk, trot and canter. Horses are able to think in halt and walk, but this thinking ability decreases in trot and becomes very difficult in canter. Horses in the wild spend most of their

Vogue was unwilling to walk through narrow gaps in hedges when we were out hacking. To change this situation I went back to the school. Here, Vogue is walking through the gaps between me and the fence in walk – I start by having the gap quite wide and as she grows in confidence I make the gap narrower – once she is really confident in walk I will increase pace until she doesn't even bat an eyelid

day in walk and grazing, and general interaction will create a bit of trot but only for a short amount of time. If a horse is in canter or gallop, he is generally fleeing something, which is an instinctive reaction that is fuelled by adrenaline and, as already mentioned, adrenaline prevents thinking and logical thought. Therefore I would teach a horse in walk and then take him through each stage until he is completely 'endorphic' (in a state where the natural relax-and-feel-good chemicals in the body, endorphins, have taken over) and able to think, even in canter. This can be taught, but always remember that you are asking huge things of your horse. It is not natural for him, but it is a testament to how amazing horses are.

Here Clemmie is walking through narrow gaps made by the barrels – Clemmie isn't worried as we have put in a lot of work previously. If these kind of exercises are neglected, you end up with a situation like Vogue and it can make for an unsafe horse

Equipment you will need

Foal slip

When a foal is young he shouldn't have any bad habits, so there is no reason to use anything other than a foal slip on him. You are not looking to pull him about, just guide him.

Horseman's halter

This is a rope halter that gives the horse clear signals because of the narrowness of the rope. A normal, broad headcollar may appear to give clear signals but it deadens down the communication and means you will probably have to exert more pressure to get the horse to understand what you are asking. I will always give young horses the benefit of the doubt and start training in a horseman's halter.

Training halter (pressure and release)

I use these halters in my everyday life on horses that need retraining as I feel it levels the playing field. Of course it's all about kidding the horse, as they could still do what they wanted if they set their mind to it, but because the level of pressure exerted is equal to the pressure they themselves put on it, they believe that you are quicker, bigger and stronger than they are. Most horses will test the halter about three times and then submit to it, enabling you to move forward with your relationship. I personally would rather a few short sessions with a training halter than spend every day wrestling with my horse. Once the horse has understood, I go back to using a horseman's halter or an ordinary headcollar.

12 foot (3.6 metre) rope

This is the minimum rope length I would use, primarily because of safety. With a 12 foot (3.6 metre) rope you can always get out of the way even if the horse rears. It will also allow you to shake the rope at him whilst he is on his back legs, rather than you disciplining him when his feet are back on the ground where they should be. For horses that bolt in hand, the 12 foot (3.6 metre) rope gives you time to get into a stance that will enable you to stop your horse; with a short rope you will find yourself being dragged along with them.

This length of rope allows me to do all my groundwork wherever and whenever needed. If I was going to loose jump or do more distance work, I would use a 22 foot (6.7 metre) rope.

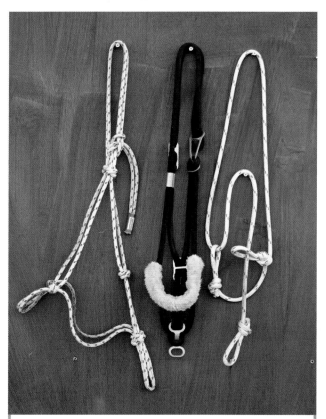

From right to left: horseman's halter, rope headcollar and a training halter based on pressure and release

From left to right: 22ft (6.7m) rope, 12ft (3.6m) rope and a pair of 32ft (9.7m) long-lines

Bridle, saddle, saddle cloth

These are self-explanatory, but I generally don't use a noseband with the bridle – there is enough for the horse to think about without having to add more to the equation. I usually choose a fulmer snaffle bit, as the cheek gives support and guidance without too much downwards pressure. The mouthpiece can be straight plastic, mullen mouth or French link.

Long-lines

I use two 32 foot (9.7 metre) lines. It is important to have them at this length so that your outside line can go round your horse and back to your hand without you having to reach for it. This will also allow for a bigger circle, which is less stressful physically.

Bits

I like to keep things simple when bitting youngsters. At the start, I use a plastic bit so that it doesn't bang against the teeth. However, once youngsters are being ridden, I find that they tend to lean on a plastic bit. It is at this stage that I move on to a hinged fulmer bit as this has a squeezing action rather than a pinch. A bit that pinches will slow down the learning and can make future bitting a problem.

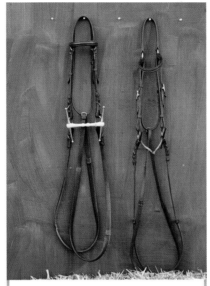

Bridles without nosebands: with plastic fulmer snaffle (left) and with hinged fulmer (right)

Saddle and saddle cloth

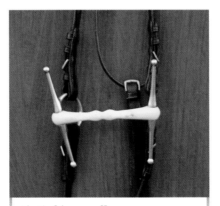

Plastic fulmer snaffle

Hinged fulmer

The orphan foal

I've already mentioned the 'tough love' aspect of owning a young horse, and if ever there's a situation where your heart strings are in danger of pulling you into the trap of sentimentality, it's with an orphan foal. Buying a youngster is one big responsibility; hand rearing an orphan is an even bigger one, and requires a special mention.

If, for whatever reason, you end up with an orphan foal, then it is really important that you understand that the future is going to be a great challenge, and it is essential to get your foal integrated with other horses. The best way to do this is to try to find a foster mother. This is where you have to do the opposite to what your human nurturing side tells you – for your foal to have the best chance of normality, it is crucial.

My experiences with hand-reared foals are very dramatic and sometimes even traumatic. The ones that I have come in contact with are often incredibly aggressive with no idea of normal equine social behaviour. I am talking about bottle-fed foals here, not foals that have been put on a foster mare.

If you do find yourself with an orphan foal, it is crucial that you integrate him with other horses as soon as you can so that he can learn how to behave like a horse and understand the pecking order. Here you can see that the older horse is keeping his eye on this young foal

It's reached the point where if I get a call regarding problems with an orphaned, bottle-fed horse, I literally get a sense of foreboding. Maybe I only hear about the ones that have gone astray, but I have found that they have little or no respect for humans and this causes them to become very dominant. When the owner realizes what has gone wrong, it is too late. I have also found that because they haven't been reared by horses, they don't behave in a way an integrated horse would, so their understanding of pressure and release isn't there. They just don't understand how horses discipline each other.

Years ago a lovely lady sent me a bottle-fed three year old, and it was one of the strangest experiences I have ever had. This youngster was so aggressive, but she would come at you over the stable door with her ears pricked and looking like she was going to give you a big hello, then she would attack you over the door with her ears still pricked forward. She had no facial expressions, so I wasn't able to read what she was going to do next.

This mare was eventually put to sleep as the risk to people was huge, and even if you had thought 'well I'll retire her to a field', if she had needed any attention, veterinary or otherwise, it would have been impossible. Although I am passionate about horses, I don't believe in risking a human life, her poor owner was distraught with worry and owning her was no pleasure. So remember this and proceed with extreme caution when you are caught in a dilemma and think you are doing a poor fluffy foal a favour.

Since then I have dealt with a number of bottle-fed foals and they have all been very similar. It's the strangest thing, working with a horse that doesn't realize it's a horse! I'm sure others have completely different experiences, so I am going to reiterate that maybe I have this view because I only get called out to the difficult ones, or maybe the ones that come right are integrated with other horses much earlier on in life.

I did a demonstration a number of years ago which focused on moving from groundwork to the ridden work. A youngster that had been backed and was destined for the eventing world was put forward as a candidate, as her owners weren't able to progress with her training since she challenged everything they asked.

I chose this mare for the demonstration because she was by one of my favourite event stallions. It was one of the hardest demos I have ever done, as the lack of respect from her was unbelievable. She didn't seem to get anything I was asking of her; she was very aggressive, very dominant and took a couple of swipes at me. I just happened to say to the owner as a bit of a joke, 'She wasn't bottle fed was she?' 'Oh yes' they replied. 'Her mother died at birth and we bottle fed and raised her.' Then her behaviour really made sense, and if I was honest, had I known this I would not have chosen her for the demo since she didn't behave as a normal horse, meaning that the demo wasn't useful to the people watching.

Just as the writing of this book was coming to a conclusion I was watching a vet programme on television. They ended up with an orphan foal as the mother had rejected him and wanted to kill him. I was relieved to hear the vet looking after the foal confirm my thoughts regarding orphan foals. He said that it was a bad situation because if such foals aren't integrated, they do generally become difficult and aggressive.

So remember, if you are going to take on an orphan foal, try your hardest to find a foster mare as it will be the best chance your foal will have of growing up into a normal individual. You have to appreciate that in the wild this foal would have died if something happened to his mother.

This young foal is mouthing to tell the older horse that he knows his place and that he isn't a threat. Orphaned foals that aren't intergrated, don't understand their place in the pecking order

RULES FOR SUCCESSFUL HAND-REARING

If you want your orphan foal to become a useful and cooperative adult, then several factors must be addressed and acted upon. Your first responsibility is to keep the foal alive and healthy. Contact either your local vet or stud farm and get some advice. A really good website is the foaling crisis bureau, which can be viewed at www.horsequest.co.uk.

First and foremost, do all you can to find a foster mare for the reasons discussed above. If you can't find a foster mare, proceed with extreme caution and remember some golden rules:

1. Where possible, do not hand feed your foal. Throughout the rearing of an orphan foal, you should take care to handle and interact with the foal as normally as you possibly can.

2. Try not to treat the foal as something special or even particularly lovable. Orphan foals often turn out to be quite aggressive because they become too 'humanized'. This really is where you have to overcome your automatic reaction to fall in love and feel sorry for him.

3. Have strict rules in place for when you interact with your foal. Playing is fun and crucial to development but only when its done in a respectful way, and what is funny or cute from a tiny foal may not be so from a strapping 16hh young horse.

Keeping entires

Continuing the subject of youngsters to be wary of, I feel quite strongly that unless a stallion is good enough to be used for breeding purposes, you shouldn't keep him entire, particularly if you are not set up to deal with him.

I do have a stallion, but not by choice – he is one of those horses that found me rather than me finding him. He is a Lusitano, and in Portugal traditionally they keep all the stallions for riding and all the mares for breeding.

When Trigo came to me he was incredibly nervous and hot but he had amazing manners and wasn't a problem in terms of keeping him on a livery yard. In the autumn/winter I can turn him out with other horses but in spring he has to be on his own as his hormones kick in.

Trigo (grey), my Luso stallion, is now really chilled and I can do anything with him. He still has character but he has learned to deal with his fears

In the autumn, winter and early spring he can be turned out with Jo, my gelding

If you decide that you want to keep your man entire, then you will need to have very clear boundaries and to be tough mentally in those early years, as if you give a stallion an inch, he will take a mile. You do not want your stallion thinking that he is the boss.

Apart from that, I train a stallion in exactly the same way as I do any other horse. You will probably find that an entire always wants to have something in his mouth, which can get very wearing. You don't want to get into that game of 'in the mouth, out of the mouth', like children that throw their dummy off the high chair, you pick it up, they throw it off again, you pick it up – you get my drift.

The other issue I find with colts is that they like to get in your personal space. Remember that you are entitled to defend yourself, not by getting aggressive, but by giving a sharp tap, dig or bump with your elbow or knee. Never use an open hand as the hand must be seen as a tool of praise, and you don't want them wondering if it praise or a smack that is coming.

I think of colts as being rather like a drunk at the office party who thinks his luck is in and that his advances are irresistible. The only way to get rid of them is to be blunt and to the point.

I have recently moved to an American barn where there is metal mesh between each box – I have had stallions in for backing and what has been noticeable is how much more content they are when they can see and touch other horses. I was even able to have two stallions together – they were so relaxed.

Wonky, a young colt, went to jump on top of me as an evasion to the rope and string. I have used my elbow to bump him, and I only have to do it the once. It's not about beating him, just a quick reminder about manners

This picture was taken about 30 seconds later; you can see that he is fine and has not been traumatized by my reaction to him jumping on me. This is why I find getting colts to stand in their own personal space is vital – it keeps them off you and avoids all that stuff!

PART 2

Creating a trainable brain

So you've decided you definitely want this youngster. You've taken a long hard look at yourself and know you can develop the self-discipline you need to make a good job of it. This is important, as the attitude of the handler counts for so much. Now let's get on with training the horse!

Benefits of an early start

From birth to six months, most foals spend all their time in a field because they are considered 'too young' for any work. Well that depends whether you are working their brain or their body! Yes, it is too early to put physical pressure on a foal, but there is a lot you can do at this influential time to develop a trainable brain in your foal that will give the two of you a head start for later.

When I decided to re-write an earlier book of mine, *From Birth to Backing*, I tried to find out what information was currently available to people, and, apart from imprinting a foal, I found little about the first six months of a young horse's life from training point of view. Is that because generally people don't consider anything they do with their foal in the first six months to be training? Or is it because most foals are left until weaning before any training takes place? I believe a careful early start saves many problems later on.

The moment a foal is born he is a wild animal with no idea that he is entering a life of domestication. His reactions and instincts will be automatic, and whilst it is important that he is allowed to be a foal, it is also important to realize that unless horse and human can work harmoniously, life will not be easy. Therefore, there has to be some training put in place to make weaning a fairer and easier transition.

Rules and boundaries

It is important to realize that there is a fine line between allowing a foal to be a foal and over handling; however, some boundaries still have to be put in place.

Now don't go thinking that just because I have used the word 'training' he will be able to do a dressage test by the time he is weaned! In an ideal world, when working with foals I use short sessions for a few days over a few weeks and then do nothing for a few months. I continue to work like this until they are mature and strong enough to cope with more. I feel this gives them the balance between the setting of boundaries and allowing the foal to be a foal.

However, as already mentioned, more and more foals are being born on livery yards and small holdings where they have to be handled in a stress-free way on a daily basis, so there has to be a little more work put in place. I feel the main threat to a foal's training on a livery yard or small holding is unruliness through over-familiarity.

You have to become your foal's leader, and in order to do this, he has to view you as a safe person to be around,

physically and emotionally. This means that when he reacts to something, you can be there to assure him that it isn't a scary monster that is going to eat him, which is a normal reaction for him to have every time you introduce something new.

Remember that horses live by the code of the survival of the fittest, and therefore you will get some foals that challenge everything you do. They aren't trying to be difficult, they are just closer to their instincts than those foals that take it all in their stride. I personally don't think it's got anything to do with the amount of handling they have, and later I will cover in more detail how imprinting at birth can help a foal that is close to his instincts cope with domestic life (see pages 52–53). This is when you have the opportunity to show him early on, when his mind is wide open, that there is nothing to fear. What you create is a horse that is close to his instincts but manageable, so you can work together rather than against each other. It makes even a difficult horse very trainable if you have his mind on your side.

Keeping your cool

Badly handled situations when dealing with foals can escalate into a full-blown argument, putting your relationship on a rocky footing. When this happens it is important that you deal with it in a correct manner so that you can both move forward. That said, it is important that you allow mistakes, remembering that these are part of the learning curve. Just don't get flustered, remain calm and keep your breathing regulated. If you allow your heart rate to go up, then the horse will think that he is justified in his reaction to the question or situation.

Remember, you are responsible for shaping your foal's future. You have to bear in mind that it takes a long time for a foal to understand what you are asking, so you must first be very clear in your requests and allow plenty of thinking time and lots of breaks as their little brains will be working

CALMING DOWN

If you feel your heart starting to race, start yawning to allow more oxygen into your lungs and slow your heart rate.

overtime and they will become mentally very tired. Also be aware of how you ask for things – sudden movements will frighten him. You need to move in a quiet but purposeful way. Remember he is a flight animal, so if you sneak around trying to be too quiet, he will be looking for the bogie man!

Personal space and respect

My pet hate is horses that climb all over me and are totally disrespectful of my personal space. Your personal space is the area immediately around you that no one but closest friends and family normally enter. It is important from a safety and a training point of view to teach a horse at a young age to respect personal space, to stand respectfully back from you and show him that he can be comfortable in his own space. You can do this with or without a halter. It has far-reaching effects as it teaches him patience and self-discipline, which in turn builds confidence. This has a knock-on effect on manners generally, such as when the horse is standing still at shows or needs to behave when out hacking.

The respect a horse has for your personal space is significant because it indicates whether you and your horse have a pupil-teacher relationship (which is what you want) or a parent-child relationship (which suggests over-familiarity and sentiment, rather than respect and leadership).

The pupil–teacher relationship encourages respect between horse and handler and the horse becomes a pleasure to be around, rather than a spoilt brat who demands attention all the time. To consolidate a respectful relationship, you must teach your horse to back out of your space and stay there. Don't be fooled if he keeps creeping back towards you for attention and think this is because he 'loves' you (or is 'joined-up') – it is actually a lack of respect, so don't reward it. Keep putting him back in his own space, using quiet repetition to get what you want. Consistency is the key.

With a horse that is really pushy, such as one that has already been spoiled or is a colt, I use the ring that we use for teaching young horses to tie up. Rather than tying an actual knot and fixing them to that point, I thread the rope through the ring and keep hold of the loose end (see pictures on pages 80–81). No matter how much your youngster tries to get in to your personal space, he can't because he'll be directed to the ring instead. I recently worked with a colt that was so rude and kept jumping on me and the normal elbow wasn't having much effect. I tied the rope through the ring and every time he went to jump on me he landed at the fence by the ring. He had such a temper tantrum that his behaviour was no longer working. After about five minutes he quit. I took the rope out of the ring and went back to working with him. He was a joy. A week later his owner contacted me to say the new behaviour was still in place and he had changed his attitude in many other areas, but if at any point he went back to his old ways, she now knew how to get him back on track.

Imprinting

I would imprint my foal as near to the birth as possible – that is, handle him and get him accustomed to my presence almost from the very first moment he opens his eyes after birth.

There is currently a great debate about imprinting being intrusive at such an early stage of a foal's existence. But when foals are born they don't know anything, and I feel it is fairer to show them what is going to be expected of them as a domesticated animal. Otherwise the day will come when you take them from their mother and put them under pressure and this will be a huge shock to their system. It would be like letting children just do as they please until the day they went to school. They would flounder and probably rebel as they would not have a clue what was going on, whereas a child that has had boundaries put in place at home and learned social skills is much happier and able to deal with the change. Like everything else we do with a young horse, success is achieved through balance.

Handling the foal's head and ears

Why imprint?

As already mentioned the current debate considers imprinting to be too intrusive at such an early age, whereas the reality is that we are breeding for the sole purpose of a foal being domesticated. It is true that in the wild the only things a foal needs to learn are to stand up, to get moving as quickly as possible and to stick to mum. But our world isn't going to be that simple for them, and the very fact that they are born into domestication means they are going to come into contact with stimuli that are totally alien to their natural instinct. If you can introduce things to them in the first few hours, weeks and months rather than at the age of three or four years, then the shock to them will be far less traumatic and, more importantly, you won't have half a tonne of horse saying no!

Imprinting offers the opportunity to introduce stimuli to the foal that he will have to experience as a domesticated horse at a time in his life where his mind is like a sponge, open to new things. It is a bit like the chicken that hatches and the first thing he sees is a duck – he doesn't know that he isn't a duck!

Ideally imprinting would be done just after the birth before the foal gets up to suckle. Even though I am a great believer in imprinting, I don't like to be too intrusive in this first instance, although I like to do the important areas such as head, feet, behind the elbows and the withers. These are perceived as the areas that are most vulnerable to predators and the ones that we are going to need access to the most.

DEFINITION: IMPRINTING

A rapid learning process by which a newborn or very young animal establishes a behaviour pattern of recognition and attraction to another animal of its own kind, or to a substitute or an object identified as the parent.

It is important to desensitize the foal to areas of his body that will have the most contact – the girth area is a good example

Now that I have put him in the foetal position, Paddy's facial expression shows how he has automatically relaxed

If that is all I achieve in that first hour, I know I have made a lot of progress. I would repeat this process over the next few days and then stop for a week or so. Some horseman that imprint introduce the halter and other stimuli at this time, but I have found that if I do a lot of handling of the head and ears, then halter and other pieces of equipment come later as a matter of course.

Respect mum

When I am imprinting, I am very aware of the mare and her feelings. I do not want to upset her, so I normally bring the foal round in front of her so that she can see him and make contact. It is not about excluding her and you don't want to come between them emotionally. She does, however, need to understand that you are going to handle her baby. In the wild this just wouldn't happen, so you are showing the mare that you mean no harm. You need to remember that some mares when they have given birth can revert back to their natural instincts and you could see behaviour that appears to be totally out of character, but if you have built solid foundations with your mare, then that shouldn't be a problem for long.

If your foal becomes anxious, use finger-tip pressure to try to contain him and fold his legs up into the foetal position, which will comfort him. You may notice that your foal starts to lick and chew at this point. Do not try to wrestle him if he becomes anxious and make the session one of panic and fear. This is another reason I like to stick to simple imprinting.

Imprinting is not about becoming over-familiar and babying a foal, it's a process of education. Foals become over-familiar very quickly, so be careful that you don't train that kind of behaviour.

With Paddy, the foal shown in these pictures, I wasn't able to begin imprinting him until he was a few hours old but I have found that this time delay doesn't have too much affect on the results. Later on in this book, you will see me work with youngsters that haven't been imprinted at all and the difficulties that leads to. The idea that we should allow the foal to be a foal and then let the young horse be a horse until he is three or four years old may need to be reconsidered as we make more and more demands on today's horse.

Halter training

It amazes me how many horses don't respect their halter. This is fundamental, as a horse that understands the halter understands pressure and release, which is the foundation of all your future training.

Horses that pull back when tied up, won't be lead properly or won't load are horses that haven't accepted their halter and haven't learned to give to pressure from a human. You really cannot proceed to a well-schooled riding horse without this basic understanding. Having a horse that respects his halter is imperative to good progressive training, and you can start very early. Foals gain strength and confidence very quickly, so it is important that you successfully halter train your youngster. It is the cornerstone of all good horsemanship, and without it you have no basis or foundation to your horse's education.

Halter training is not just about being able to lead to and from the field; a horse has to learn to give to pressure in whatever form that takes through his whole life as a domesticated horse, whether in hand or being ridden.

Allowing your youngster to run wild will ultimately make his future life much more difficult. If you have left halter training a bit late, then you might find your youngster wants to put up more of a fight, and the pressure halter would be my preference in these circumstances. It will still be better to work through this training at this stage than wait until he is three times the size and three times as strong, because you will, at some point, have to deal with this unwanted behaviour. If it is not dealt with, you will find yourself in a position where you have to use such tools as a chifney to control your horse. These items of equipment do far more damage to a horse's mouth than a halter could ever do and therefore it is not an ideal situation.

Working on instinct

I have already mentioned that although you are choosing a more natural approach to training your foal, there is still nothing natural to a foal about wearing a halter and being lead independently of mum, so you are still going to get some extreme reactions. He may well jump or try to get away from you, but he is only doing what comes naturally to him. All he knows is that you are a predator, you still have to prove to him that you really are a friend and mean him no harm. The most important thing to remember in these situations is to remain calm and regulate your breathing. You may find your foal will press his muzzle near your wrist, and I believe when he does this, he is checking your heart rate! He wants to know that you are cool, calm and collected, as this will cause him to worry less; if your heart rate is up, you are telling him that there *is* something to worry about. So remain calm and allow him to work things out. Only ever use finger-tip control to contain him; never get into a battle or punish him for reacting in an instinctive way but equally do not allow him to control your reaction. Do not teach him that when he behaves in such a manner you will back off, just quietly persist with your task. He will quickly realize that it is his responsibility to find the comfort zone.

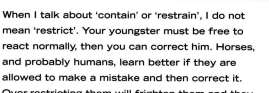

RESTRAINT AND CONTAINMENT

When I talk about 'contain' or 'restrain', I do not mean 'restrict'. Your youngster must be free to react normally, then you can correct him. Horses, and probably humans, learn better if they are allowed to make a mistake and then correct it. Over-restricting them will frighten them and they will shut down mentally; at this age it will be a hard task to win them back around. However, you are only human and if you do make the odd mistake, don't dwell on it, just move forward.

Early halter training

Taking hold of a foal until he has given up the fight is one possibility at this age, but it is not one that I recommend. We want to train willing minds, and this young age is the ideal opportunity to show a foal that if he allows us to guide, influence and direct him with a halter, his life will be much easier and more secure.

In my opinion, a mistake that we commonly make is wanting to lead our foal in straight lines from day one – but that is the end result, not the beginning. We often resort to showing him that if he does not not follow we can make it a little uncomfortable for him by bending him and forcing

him a little off balance to prevent him from 'planting'. It is natural for a foal to get stuck when asked this question about leading and it is our natural reaction to pull him round. But if we are patient and wait, walking in a straight line won't take long but it will have to be repeated more than once before he gets it.

Before we get started, remember that asking a foal to turn away from his mother, even when she is so close, is very emotionally challenging and it is better to keep the sessions short. On the first day I won't expect to be able to lead a foal independently, but I would start the process.

HOW TO ... INTRODUCE EARLY HALTER TRAINING

Here we have Manny, an 11-day-old foal that has not been imprinted. Although he wears a halter, he has no idea what this halter means. Ideally, I would have started this work much earlier and in the stable, but life sometimes dictates otherwise. Better late than never!

Manny was quite a handful even for a normal foal. He has been bred on a livery yard where he has to be brought in and out of the field through the yard and past other horses. Foals must be handled frequently but in a manner that doesn't encourage over-familiarity and generally bolshy behaviour

I start by asking Manny to come off pressure by walking in a semi-circle and inviting him to come, without taking a direct pull. He is wearing a foal slip but it doesn't mean anything to him yet (at this age all schooling can be done in a foal slip). I need to show him that there is a direct relationship to the halter and the handler

It became apparent to me that although he has had a lot of handling, he was worried about me being above him. As Manny was worried by my height, I came down to his level whilst I was schooling him. Notice that I haven't had to close my hand round the rope, I only use thumb and finger pressure to take a feel on the rope, then take a slight bend and with quiet softness – I say what I mean and mean what I say

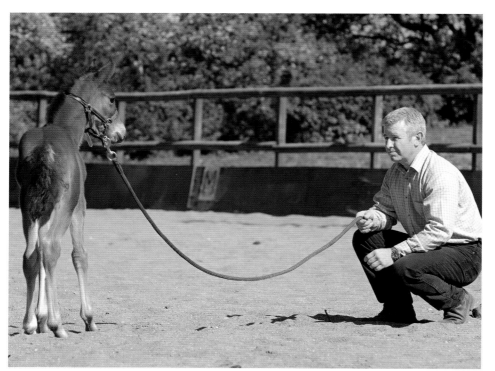

As soon as he turned his quarters out and looked at me, I released the feel on the rope. Notice the quizzical look – even at this age Manny is digesting that it is easier to give to pressure, and at this point it can be tempting to pull the foal around and to use more pressure rather than keeping an even feel and allowing it to work.

Here Manny has balked at the situation, which he is fully entitled to do, but notice I have not grabbed hold of him. I have allowed my arm to move forward but I am still only applying minimal pressure. This can quite often happen if mum calls to her foal, and although I have only used minimal pressure, it is still important to not let the foal get away from me. I may have to move my feet a bit quicker and stay with him.

When a foal has been through a period of pressure, he can become a little flighty, even when everything has been going well for a few repetitions, so at this point it may be prudent to make contact. He will then start to enjoy the sensation of you touching him, but it is important to not over fuss him at this stage. Once you have made contact go back to work.

This sequence of pictures shows how Manny has gone from being quite wary to over-familiar in a matter of seconds. At this stage I wouldn't do too much about this, but it has shown me that Manny will be easy to train and that he learns very quickly. If you are wondering how you would correct this behaviour, then let me reassure you that by the time you have finished putting these principles in place, you will have a foal that is respectful and this behaviour will be in the past without you even realizing it.

Curious

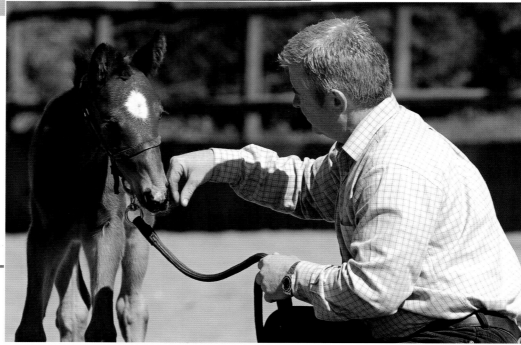

More curious

Very inquisitive

Very over-familiar

Here I am getting Manny to softly yield his quarters. Again, notice that I am only using two fingers on the rope and my hand on his rump; this uses two points of guidance which can prevent panic and 'sitting down', which can happen when only using one point of pressure (for example the halter). All I want Manny to achieve in this session is to yield to the pressure of a halter and to turn and face me, which is what he would do if mum put visual pressure on him.

Foals get tired quickly so allow plenty of breaks and let them suckle.

In this first short session I taught Manny that there was a direct link between his halter and the person on the other end of it. He still isn't leading in straight lines, but that will come over the next couple of sessions. Remember to work towards your end goal gradually – don't expect the foal to get it all in one short session. Did you sit your exams after only one day at school?

Here Manny feels comfortable enough to scratch his neck with his hind leg, for me that is a great sign that he is ok with what I am asking of him.

Leading

This is Manny's second session. In the first I taught him that there was a direct relationship between the halter and me, his handler, but I still haven't taught him to lead in a straight line. Most horse owners take it for granted that their horses will lead in a straight line, so when they either breed or buy a youngster, they are surprised when the youngster doesn't understand the concept.

Now you may be one of the lucky people that has a youngster that just seems to know what he is doing, but that is quite often a fluke and your control will be put to the test when something unexpected happens.

DON'T TRAIN A ONE-SIDED HORSE

A good tip is to practise leading on both the nearside and the offside. When Manny had his outburst I was on his off side, which is probably what sparked off his tantrum, but it is really important to not have a one-sided horse. Time spent on this area of training will reap dividends for you and your relationship in the future, so do tackle it now.

HOW TO ... INTRODUCE LEADING

To start the session I am going to make sure that Manny remembers about pressure, so that if something happens and he runs to the end of the rope he knows to stop, turn to face me and come forward so the rope becomes slack. If he keeps going back, I don't stand there and pull at his head; instead, I will maintain the pressure on the rope and walk with him. The object isn't to force him to come forward but wait until he makes the decision to.

I am going to start leading Manny using a horseman's string placed around his quarters. I don't want to drag my foal around by the head to teach him to lead, I want to guide him using two points of pressure. In addition, this is the very beginning of desensitizing your young horse to other things around his back end such as a fillet string on a rug, or long-lines.

To get Manny going I will set him off on a circle and then begin to zigzag. Eventually, I will be looking to lead him in a straight line as my control improves.

The reaction, above, is totally normal and you will see it a lot when you first start working with your foal. The point to remember is to not jerk them about as this will worry them more; just keep a constant pressure on the rope until they come back to you.

Here I have my fingers in Manny's foal slip as well as the rope around his quarters. I am using this to show Manny that I walk my line and he walks his, which keeps him in his own space and out of mine. This is a great lesson to teach now, as one of the biggest problems I see in the 'terrible twos' (see pages 90–91) is your youngster walking across in front of you. So I am keeping his body straight and using my hand in his foal slip to keep his nose away from me.

The picture (left) was taken just a few moments later and as you can see Manny isn't at all traumatized, so don't beat yourself up if your youngster goes all dramatic, chucks themself on the floor and completely overreacts!

Manny is now leading in a very forward manner and has taken responsibility for keeping the rope slack. This isn't the finished article and Manny will have backwards steps, so this needs to be re-done for several days until he leads straight off every time I clip a rope on his halter.

Basic handling

This section provides a detailed look at all of the handling skills you will need in daily life with your foal, but to start with, spend as much time as you can covering vulnerable areas, including the head, belly and feet. Before you start working these areas make sure that all the previously mentioned work is in place and you are happy that your youngster understands the principle of coming off the halter pressure and that he has started to respect personal space. Three consecutive days of this type of work, every month or so, will stand you in good stead for weaning and thereafter.

Handling feet

It's a good idea to handle your youngster's feet from day one, picking them up and patting them, and also handling them in preparation for the farrier, that is, putting the horse's leg into the position needed for trimming. Although your foal isn't going to see the farrier for sometime, get him used to the way his feet will be handled, rather than leading him into a false sense of security and making the first farrier visit a nightmare situation instead of just another thing that he has to go through as a domesticated horse.

Only start this task once your youngster is fully halter trained. I start this exercise at the end of a successful session leading around mum in the school or field. This way my youngster has done a bit of work and his brain is in a relaxed state.

HOW TO ... HANDLE FEET

I always start with my 12 foot (3.6m) rope to help me in this exercise. This allows me to work from a distance, as the early stages of picking your youngster's feet brings you too far underneath him and encourages him to lean on you. By using the rope your youngster has to learn to balance himself.

Once your youngster is fine with you picking his foot up with the rope, try pulling it up and forward. You may get a reaction where he goes up slightly, but remain calm and repeat the exercise until it is no big deal.

It is only when you can repeat the previous exercise without any hiccups that you can move onto handling his feet yourself. Remain at a safe distance and start by keeping the rope on his foot. As you ask him to lift with the rope, run your hand down the rope to the foot. Once you feel comfortable doing that, you can move on to direct contact with the foot. Because I work with so many horses, I can achieve this in one session, but you may find that it takes a couple of sessions with the rope before you feel comfortable about picking the feet up yourself.

Repeat the previous exercises with your foal's hind feet and again don't panic if he tries to resist. This is normal behaviour for a youngster. If you want to, you can break the sessions up into front feet and hind feet, with the final goal being to do both in the same session.

Vulnerable areas

While your foal is young and still a good height for handling, do yourself a massive favour and start to work on vulnerable areas such as the belly. Make it fun and use it as part of a grooming exercise. In the next section you will encounter a weanling that has a real problem about his owner handling him in a number of areas, especially his head and neck. Had this been tackled when he was younger it would have saved a lot of trouble.

The key areas I like to work with are a foal's head and ears, belly, withers and feet. When you first work on these areas, you will find that your youngster is very wary as every nerve in his body tells him to *not* let you anywhere near these vulnerable places. Keep a finger in his headcollar and go with him as he tries to move away, keeping your hand on the area you are working with not allowing him to shake you off. As soon as he stands still, take your hand away as a reward and keep repeating the exercise until he accepts your touch without question. However, if you have been able to imprint, you will find that you don't get negative reactions. I would still use these exercises regularly even on imprinted youngsters.

Weaning: a key experience

I believe that getting weaning right is *the* most important aspect of breeding a youngster. Many people get fixated with backing, but that is relatively minor compared to a traumatized youngster that is suffering from separation anxiety.

The magic age for weaning seems to be about six months but this is the absolute earliest I would wean. Both of my youngsters were fully weaned at nine months, and by allowing them this extra time I was able to stretch that strong bond between mare and foal rather than break it.

Having more than one youngster so you can wean them together is the ideal; however, if you are not in that situation, you can still make it a very successful transition, and doing all the work I talk about in this section will go a long way to helping you to wean your foal successfully. The work all centres around the foal becoming independent of his mum.

First day at school

A child that spends most of his time with a parent and doesn't go to pre-school classes is the one you will see hysterically clinging to his mum's leg on the first day of school! Mum is probably also crying and is traumatized, and the child is left feeling abandoned. This can affect how the child sees school for the rest of his life. Make sure your foal isn't this traumatized child! If you follow the basic outline in this section, by the time he is four months you will be able lead your foal independently of his mum, work in and around his vulnerable areas, pick up his feet and do anything else that you have introduced him to. Then you can start thinking about working the mare and foal around each other.

Daily routine

It is imperative at this age that your mare and foal are not left unattended, so this requires two people.

As part of your routine, when you bring your foal in, start to work with the mare and the foal together. Start with the foal standing in the middle and the mare walking around him, then the other way round. Go on to walking them both on a circle but in opposite directions, making the circle bigger and bigger as they become more confident. This teaches them to cope with leaving each other and passing again.

Even at this young age, by working with your foal and getting him to walk around his mum, his confidence builds and you will find that makes weaning a much easier transition. Doing this every time you work with your foal for two or three minutes will make all the difference

The reason I weaned my foals at nine months was so that over the months this exercise could be done over a much larger area where the mare and foal actually went out of sight of each other, starting with short periods of a minute or so and building up to five or ten minutes.

You will be amazed at how quickly the foal's confidence will grow and the bond between mother and foal will start to stretch. When you start to see this, you can then think about putting them in separate stables. Again, start this transition

small by beginning with a few minutes in the afternoon, with mum tied up or perhaps being groomed outside. Have the foal in the stable so that he can touch his mum over the door. Make sure that until you feel confident that the foal won't try to jump over the stable door, there is someone in there with him and that he is wearing a halter and rope.

Separable friends

I was lucky enough to have two weanlings so they did everything together, but I always worked them independently so that they didn't get attachment problems. For example, although they lived in the same field, I didn't bring them in together when it was time to do some work.

This was a deliberate move on my part so that they got used to the other going away and coming back. When I started to stretch the bond, I would put the youngsters in a stable together with their mums on either side for an hour in the afternoon after a period of work. I then stretched this arrangement to over night (because I had left them until they were that bit older, they were beginning to naturally wean themselves).

It got to the point where I could leave the weanlings in the stable and take mum away to work for a short period. Then one day when they were about nine months old, I popped both mares in the boxes around the corner and I didn't get one night of calling. They all lived on the same property for a couple of years and I never had any issues. The youngsters stayed together but I always brought them in separately to work, and I never had any calling or napping problems between them.

Doing lots of exercises over short periods of time throughout that first six to nine months works the same way as a parent with a child – it builds the youngster's confidence, meaning that they are ready for the world and when the day comes to go to school, it's no big deal

BRINGING MUM BACK INTO WORK

If your mare needs to come back into work while her foal is still at foot, get someone to hold her foal in the school and work around them. There is no reason why you cannot ride the mare. I remember as a child going show jumping and seeing a mare do her round with her foal waiting in the collecting ring with a handler, neither mare nor foal were worried or shouting for each other. The key point to remember is that we are gradually trying to stretch the bond between mare and foal, not break it abruptly and traumatically.

Questions and answers

Q My filly is nearly six months old now and I have been doing a bit of rope work with her. She leads reasonably well and will move her shoulders and quarters when asked, back up nicely and I can pop the rope over her head and get her to turn around and have the rope around her tummy and quarters without any problem. She will tie up and stand well. However, she gets very bothered when it comes to anything new such as poles on the ground or cones – she is really unhappy about even walking past them, never mind over them.

A You say that she leads 'reasonably' well, but I would like you to get her to be leading *very* well. Then go back to the situation and put yourself between the obstacles and the foal so that you can keep her moving, and keep doing that until she is more settled and you can put her next to the obstacle.

As you have said that you can move her shoulders and quarters, you must use this to your advantage. It is common when a foal's handler comes up against a problem that they have a knee-jerk reaction of grabbing hold of the rope and the horse's head and then they get into a stand-off situation. What I would suggest is that you use the groundwork by getting her to move her shoulders, move her quarters and keep going in that vein. You will find that eventually she will be so tuned into what you are asking that she will forget to get worried by the new things.

Q I like my mare and foal to live out 24/7 as much as possible. Should I rug my foal, and if so, how do I go about introducing the rug without panicking him?

I personally will only rug a foal to keep them dry, as wet foals will lose weight and can get a chill. If the conditions are just cold, then I wouldn't rug as a rule.

However, I would make sure my foal would accept a rug as part of his education so that if the situation arises, I am not left with a foal that is stressed. I would do this as part of his desensitization and start as I did with Wonky using a small piece of folded up plastic that is gradually opened out to a rug. Many foals don't need to go through this process and actually accept a rug very easily. You know your foal and if he gives you the feeling that he may be spooky about it and become stressed, then the exercises in this book will help you enormously.

Many foal/horse owners find that it is the leg straps that worry them the most, never mind the foal. This is where you really see the benefits of imprinting and doing the rope work, as all this deadens down the sensation of the rope around their legs and quarters.

Q How should I travel a foal on his own? Would you travel him tied up? He has never been tied up before and will not be before then as he is living out at stud until I pick him up.

A Ideally you would have taught him to tie up and the best way to do this is using the ring and a long rope passed through the ring to the headcollar so that it moves freely (see pages 80–81). However, as you have not yet taught him to tie up, I would travel him loose without a partition. If there is a breast bar in the front I would use straw bales so that he can't get underneath them. I would also put straw bales at the back of the trailer as it is the accelerating and decelerating that can cause him to move about and become worried.

Q My youngster gets very stressed if not turned out first, and pulls and jogs all the way to the field. She's 16hh+ and still growing. How do I calm her behaviour and gain control?

A This really is a chicken and egg situation as the groundwork should improve the turning out situation, this scenario tells me that there is a possibility your horse doesn't truly respect the halter and what you are asking. She needs to learn that there is a direct link between the halter and rope and you as the handler.

If you are ground training after turnout and it still isn't improving the situation with the turnout, then you have to look at how you are asking your horse. Self-discipline from the horse only comes with self-discipline from the handler.

This period of training will make both of you uncomfortable whilst going through it because you will both have to come out of your comfort zones in order to get this problem dealt with.

Although your horse gets stressed, she will always be that way if you do not work through it and help her to realize that you are not hurting or killing her. This is where you have to be quietly persistent.

For you this is the pivotal point of dealing with stress in your horse in every eventuality. If you don't come through this, your horse will be stressed about every new situation, and stressed horses become very difficult to be around. You may have to show some tough love here.

You don't say how old your youngster is, but if she is old enough to introduce a bridle, I would try a different type of groundwork – don't just do circling work, do more slower lateral work which will get her to think rather than rush around on a circle.

To summarize, you need to mean what you say, be clear in your asks, don't start what you can't finish and get help if you feel that you can't do it on your own.

When you are starting lateral work, use a fence line. When your youngster has got the hang of it, you can start to work across the school

By doing close lateral work not only will you get her attention but you are teaching her to bend her neck, which really helps with horses that are difficult to lead as you can teach them to yield

Q When I started to work my youngster on a 12 foot (3.6 metre) line he was quite responsive but now he is sluggish and I find it hard to get him to move.

A Most horses that are sluggish to move are not being asked correctly in their mind. This is where you really have to watch your body positioning, and the accuracy in which you spin your rope. I'll give you a scenario. One of the liveries on the yard has started to ground train her horse – he is a good all-rounder and shouldn't present any problems. However, after a couple of days she asked me to help as her horse wasn't reacting as he was in the lesson – he had become sluggish and dismissive.

I watched her work and could see straight away that her horse was only reacting to what she was asking of him, which to be fair wasn't much.

The sending away is the most important aspect, the circle will be better the more effective that is, and you can't expect to improve the circle if your horse goes off half heartedly or explosively.

Checklist for sending away

- Hold your arm out to ask for the direction of travel. Whilst holding your arm out you need to keep a very positive feel on your horse's head. (You can lessen this as your horse becomes established.)
- Then you need to drive him on to the circle using your rope but make sure you spin towards his nose as you face him. Remember you are supposed to be creating visual pressure; your horse will know if you are spinning your rope towards him or not. You may find this difficult if you are used to lungeing, as with lungeing you may find that you move more to get your horse to move.
- Remember to change what you are doing every three to four circles, whether it is a change of direction or change of pace.

You can see here that the rope is very haphazard and isn't directed between the horse's shoulder and nose – your youngster will know this

If you are struggling with the rope and you aren't getting control, then tie the rope to the fence and imagine you have a horse in front of you. Aim to spin the rope between his shoulder and his nose

Q I have tried to do circling work with my youngster but he keeps turning to face me uninvited. How do I get him to stop doing this?

A This is actually quite common. It shows two things: the first is over-familiarity, as your horse is thinking that 'mum doesn't really mean for me to go away and work' and secondly that a clever horse has worked out what you are going to ask and starts to pre-empt you. Whichever the reason, you will deal with it in the same way – it just might take a bit longer with the over-familiar horse and he may get a little disgruntled at you suddenly becoming bossy.

The disadvantage of allowing your youngster to become over-familiar is that when it is time to train, you have to show some tough love, which can sometimes leave you feeling a bit upset as you are now out of your comfort zone. However, your horse isn't feeling upset, so don't put human emotions onto him. It is important that you work through it.

I would train youngsters in a horseman's halter, but if they become rude or ignore me when using it, then I will move to use a pressure halter as it speeds up the line of communication and the 'ask' becomes clearer to the horse. I can then get back to softer asks. The main philosophy in my training is to always work back to the softer – less is more.

To solve the problem you need to be alert and ready to react and correct him when he turns in. Correct him by repeating the process you used to get him to go away in the first place. You will find that he will want to sulk and ignore you, but keep up the pressure until he does as he has been asked. The first few times he will probably look like he's about to have a bit of a tantrum. That doesn't matter as it will become less and less. He will still keep trying to turn in early, but stick to your guns and the full circle will eventually come. This is where patience and determination will win the day.

There are a couple of things going on here. Monty is a really laid-back horse but he quietly controls the relationship between himself and his owner. He is disgruntled that mum is now being a bit bossy and asking more from this relationship. His foot striking out is Monty being annoyed, but also the rope isn't actually directed toward Monty's shoulder, so he really doesn't believe that mum means what she says. However, mum did mean it and Monty did do as he was asked and there has been a knock-on effect in his behaviour when hacking out. Now when mum says it's fine and the windmill isn't going to get you he trusts her and they are now really enjoying hacking out.

When he turns in to face you without being asked, you really have to be ready and quick off the mark to correct him. Here Monty has gone off, but in a bit of a strop – don't worry about this at this stage. If you mean what you say your horse will eventually realize that his behaviour isn't changing anything and that it is easier to do as asked

Q When I am doing my circling work I find that once I have asked my youngster to stop and turn in to face me, she won't stand in her own space and creeps towards me. I then find that I end up backing away from her. How do I go about correcting this behaviour?

A It is definitely a problem that you need to sort out because as long as your horse can get you to back out of your space, she will be in control of your relationship. It is because of this that a lot of horses don't like to back up. She is also creeping back towards you because she doesn't believe that you mean what you say.

To correct this you need to be alert. When I say alert, I mean watch out for it happening. Many times I watch owners with their horses and they haven't noticed that their horse has started to creep until the horse is right at their side, which is hilarious from the horse's point of view as they have given loads of warning and the handler has ignored them – 'one point' to the horse.

So next time you work your horse and you ask her to turn in, be alert. The minute she steps one foot towards you, shake the rope at her – not violently, just a gentle shake as if to say 'no you don't'. If she still comes towards you then shake the rope again, but if she persists in coming, then you can really shake it at her as you have asked politely twice. The next time she tries it shake, gently again. If she ignores you, then again up the level of pressure.

I find that most horses get it really quickly if they believe you mean it. Once you have got her standing in her own space quietly ask her to back up.

As soon as you see your youngster start to creep, wiggle the rope at them. It is not about smacking them round the face with the rope; it should be just enough to get their attention. Only up the level of pressure if they are completely ignoring you

This session has only taken 3–4 minutes at the most and Sally is learning to stand in her own space and to be comfortable there. She will learn that when the rope is on the floor, it is time out and time to chill. This is really important if you want a horse that you can take to shows or even on day trips out and about as you won't want them to jump on you all the time

PART 3

Preparing for a working life

One of the most popular questions that I am asked by the owners of young horses is, 'What can I do with them once they are weaned and before backing, without putting any strain on their joints and spoiling them?' Well the answer to that is, 'Loads, but you don't have to do it all every day.'

I use this time with youngsters to 'prepare' them for their future; for example, later in this section I cover 'preparation for loading' but I don't actually take the horse into a trailer! You won't load at this point, but there are lots of things that you can do to help prepare them for that day.

STOP! DON'T BE HASTY

You may have opened this book at this page without reading the first two parts because you have bought a weanling and think that you don't need to know the foal information. The chances are, however, that your weanling won't have had any foundations put in place. So before you start work with your youngster, go through this checklist.

1. Does he respect your personal space?
2. Does he understand that his halter means something?
3. Does he respond to pressure in whatever form it takes?
4. Can you lead him in a straight line in a calm manner?
5. Does he allow basic handling such as around his feet, head and ears?

If your answer to some of these questions is 'no', then take heart that it is never too late and you can go back and introduce these elements before you start anything else.

The next stage

I have two rules of thumb that I like to stick to. My first is that if I am introducing a horse to something new, I like to work for three days back to back, and then turn the horse away again for a few weeks or a month. When they come back in, I will go over the last session and introduce something new, again doing this for three days and then back out again.

My second rule is that because young horses between the ages of 18 and 30 months (teenage years) will have tantrums, I don't introduce anything new in that time, I only go over things that they already know. I use the time to consolidate the earlier teaching and concentrate on discipline and consistency. It just saves on all those confrontational moments.

Remember that your horse is still young and his ability to concentrate will be short, so two 20-minute sessions a day for three days will be better than a one hour session per day.

If you manage to cover all of the areas in this section with your youngster successfully before introducing the tack and rider, you will find that even the process of backing and riding away becomes just another day and it will all be uneventful, avoiding those situations that can make backing a youngster a nightmare for everyone concerned.

Before you start

Make sure your halter work is up to scratch (see pages 54–61). When I want to introduce something new to a horse, whether they are a youngster or an older horse, I first have to make sure that my halter work is excellent so that the horse understands what is happening when I put him under pressure. If I am going to ask him to do something that may cause a reaction, I will always introduce it after a period of work. When a horse has been working using the left side of his brain, he will be in a much better position mentally to cope with anything new and it will help him to think more logically about what you are asking. This means you are less likely to get a reaction.

REHABILITATING THE OLDER HORSE

Although I have used the following exercises on a young horse, they can be implemented anytime you feel you need to train or retrain your horse, regardless of his age. So this is where you start if you had a ten-year-old with a loading or clipping problem, for example. You can still use all the same information and techniques, it just might take longer and the horse will obviously be bigger and stronger, so be careful that you don't get railroaded and that your groundwork is excellent.

Reading your horse

When you are working with and introducing new things to your horse, there are lots of signs I want you to look out for. These are really important as they will let you know what your horse is going through.

- When you first start to work with your horse, his lower lip will probably be quite tight. You are looking for him to loosen his lower lip, gulp, and lick and chew, which will show you that he is thinking about and processing the information. I always release any pressure, whether it is visual or tactile, and if you want to, you can rub your horse at this point to show him that you have understood that he is trying to work things out.
- The other thing to watch out for is lowering of the head. Horses that feel adrenalized will raise their heads in preparation to take off; once they feel relaxed and more emotionally comfortable they will start to lower their head.
- Expert opinion varies on this, but I think that if a horse develops a hanging lower lip while you are working with him, it means that they have the potential to have a big tantrum and I have to say it has never failed me. If I'm working on a loading problem and the horse I am working with suddenly looks like they have a big pet lip, I know that I am going to get an explosion and I can prepare myself and the horse so that no one gets hurt. But it is these types of horses that are more likely to throw themselves on the floor.

In this picture I am getting Wonky used to something being above him – he has raised his head and has tightened his lower jaw. This is to be expected as he is worried and he's also used to getting his own way

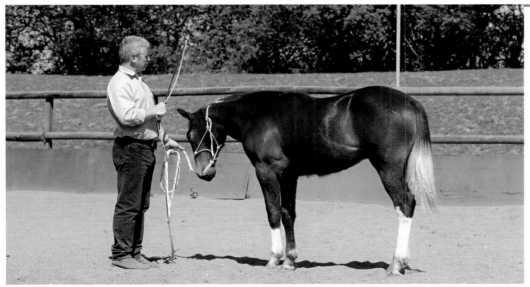

Wonky is now so relaxed that not only is his head lower and his mouth relaxed but he also goes to play with the rope – all good signs

SAFETY FIRST

Make sure that you do *all* your work on a safe surface as horses often don't show their true personality until they are put under pressure. To move forward you do have to deal with it, but just make sure you keep yourself and your horse safe by being quietly persistent.

Further halter training

Up to now we have only done very basic halter work with our foal but as he gets bigger and stronger, or if you have bought an unhandled youngster, you need to put boundaries in place so that he knows absolutely that you understand his language of pressure and release.

When I start halter training I begin with a pressure halter. It's not about being tougher, it's about being clearer in what I am asking, so there are no grey areas. Once I have achieved this, then I can go back to the horseman's halter, which gives the same feel as the pressure halter.

By using the pressure halter, the pressure is evenly distributed around the horse's head and the amount of pressure exerted is according to how much the horse resists. This is why it is so effective and much clearer in its message. Only once or twice have I come across a horse that tries the halter out more than a couple of times. The flip side to this is that as soon as the horse does give to the pressure, it releases immediately and there is absolutely no pressure. By having such extremes, the horse very quickly learns that by coming to you, away from the pressure and keeping the rope slack, there is no pressure and everything is done quietly and efficiently.

1 Using a pressure halter and a 12 foot (3.6m) rope, I put myself about 6 feet (1.8m) away from Gwin, a Fresian filly, take up the slack in the rope and apply a small amount of pressure. Gwin at this point will do one of two things: she will either step forward off the pressure and come towards me, but this is unlikely, or she will take up the pressure and move backwards. If she does the latter, I will not apply more pressure but will walk with her maintaining the same amount of pressure. At some point she will stop and work out what she needs to do.

2 In this next picture you can see that it actually took Gwin only a short time to work out that she needed to come forward. As soon as she did, the pressure was released. Not all horses are as quick as this but Gwin is really bright and picks everything up pretty fast. The important point now is to keep repeating the exercise until she gets to the point where she sees me go to take up the slack and comes forward. If you observe your horse, he will start to watch the rope and learn that it is his job to keep the rope slack regardless of where you go. This exercise will give you the ultimate horse in terms of leading regardless of the direction you take.

3 Gwin's owner, Claire, wants to show her but Gwin has never lead very easily and when it comes to trotting up, Claire couldn't get her to trot at her shoulder. Using the principle that I have just taught her, I can teach her to trot up. With the halter on, I started by marching off, as you can see she got left behind, but she now knows that it is her job to keep the slack in the rope.

4 It took a couple of minutes for her to get the idea and she was soon trotting up at my shoulder. These principles really are a good tool and can help in a huge number of areas.

5 To help Gwin become more confident and extravagant, I have put her on a circle and then asked her to come off the circle in a straight line. As you can see she is getting more and more confident, and it won't take Claire long to get Gwin trotting up and wowing all the judges. These processes are about showing the horse's character off, not suppressing it.

Tying up

A horse that won't tie up is one of those annoying situations that we often don't bother to correct – generally because we don't know how to correct it. The old-fashioned way was to swing a horse, which means to tie him to a fixed object and let him fight it until he gives up and learns to stand. But this is not what we want to do as it can cause all sorts of physical problems as well as trust issues. A much easier and more effective way is to use the tools you have already given your horse by applying the principles of move off pressure.

1 Here we have set up the situation to teach Wonky to tie up so that if he gets a fright he won't pull back and break away. I have threaded my rope through the ring and it is attached to Wonky's halter. This will allow me to control the situation.

2 Now I create a stimulus that gives Wonky enough of a fright to pull back. In this picture I am going to hit the boards with the end of my rope and then allow Wonky to pull back about three feet, letting the rope run through the ring. Once he has gone back about three feet, I will keep a constant feel on the rope.

The equipment needed is a large ring tied to either a wall or fence, a headcollar (I prefer a horseman's halter) and a minimum 12 foot (3.6m) rope

3 Here Wonky has reached the end of the rope and is thinking about the situation, he knows that it feels familiar as we have already done our halter work.

5 This is a good picture of Wonky having completed what was requested and he is licking and chewing, showing that he is calm and more relaxed.

4 Wonky immediately comes off the pressure and steps forward. This is where you start to see the benefits of all the training that is done as the foundations.

6 I have repeated this process using different things to cause Wonky to react until he stops reacting. He is now quite happy in his own space. If something were to happen to cause him to react, he is entitled to pull back but as soon as he takes the slack out of the rope and feels the headcollar, he should automatically come forward off the pressure.

Providing his owner goes over all these tips when she gets home, she can be confident that the next time Wonky is tied up to the trailer at a show and gets a fright, should he pull back, he will come forward off the pressure once the slack has been taken up.

OLDER HORSES

Although we have previously done this exercise with a weanling, the same principles can be used with any horse at any age. Again, to be able to teach the horse we have to set it up so that the horse learns the required behaviour.

Desensitization

So far, we have mainly covered the basic manners and daily handling of the young horse. Next he needs to learn to accept the presence of equipment such as tack and rugs, and to become familiar with other aspects of handling that will contribute to his welfare such as clipping and worming.

In this six months to three years old stage, I want to prepare my youngster for what he is going to experience when he is older; for example, I don't want to clip my unridden youngster but I can prepare him for that day. I don't necessarily want to put a bridle on my youngster but again there are things I can do to prepare him. It's the same with loading, hacking, worming and all the rest. As well as the practical aspects, there are other good reasons why you should impose these mental tests and exercises on your young horse.

Yes, I use tarpaulin and other scary things, but this isn't where I start – I would begin densensitization work by using a training stick and a horseman's string

Tuning in to sense

Horses, by the mere fact they are born flight animals, run most of the time using the right side of their brain as described earlier; in the wild, they rely on this to keep them safe and well. A domesticated horse doesn't need to worry about the same matters, but telling him that won't help. We actually have to show him how to cope and teach him to use the left side of his brain and to think.

None of us want a brain-dead mechanical horse, and training shouldn't be about getting rid of the essence of the horse. I just want a horse to be able to stop and think, which in turn will make him safer. Anyone that gets a fright is entitled to jump, and I would be concerned if there was no reaction, but what I don't want is for panic to set in and for the horse to run off blindly. To achieve this with a long-term positive effect, you have to get your horse to face his fear, to go through all the reactions and to come out the other side thinking 'well I'm still here and I can cope'. It is not about trying to teach him not to be frightened at all; it is about getting him to cope with the emotions that fear brings and how to get past it.

I have been in a situation where I have been working with a horse and the owner has said 'you're frightening him' but if he doesn't go through that and sees that he can come out of the other side just fine, he will always be frightened.

A human can rationalize (e.g. that tiny spider can't really hurt me…), whereas it isn't in a horse's nature to do that. He has to learn through experience.

Stimulating emotion

When a horse panics, it is because something has set off his panic button. That something could be visual or audible, and by using the training stick and string as follows you can create emotions to both visual and audible stimuli.

Start by having your horse in a horseman's halter, unless you know that he will run off – in which case I would recommend using a halter based around pressure and release and a 12ft (3.6m) rope. Desensitization should always be done in a controlled environment.

When I desensitize a horse, I am looking to stimulate him using both visual and audible stimuli, and I think it's important to know how your horse is going to react to something when you are least expecting it. It is no good thinking that everything is fine and then getting a violent reaction the first time you put a saddle on or long lines behind your horse.

You will need to put your horse under some form of pressure so that you know what he is capable of in an uncontrolled environment such, as traffic or birds flying up in front of him.

The form of desensitizing that I go through will help you in so many areas that you will be shocked, especially so at the fact that such a simple process can have such an amazing ripple effect.

Welcome resignation

At this point I need to explain the use of a word that seems to get horse people very emotive. That word is 'resigned'. When introducing something new to your horse that he either doesn't like or understand, he will generally go through several levels of avoidance but will at some point give up the behaviour. He will be resigned to the fact that he isn't getting away with it. He won't have 'accepted' yet, that will come as he realizes his behaviour is having positive effects and that life is becoming easier. The biggest mistake we make when working with our youngsters/horses is to quit at the point of resignation, thinking you have ended on a good note, whereas the winning key is to continue until you have acceptance. You can tell the difference by watching your horse's posture and body language.

Why have I explained this? Well, people hate the thought that their horses have to go through this feeling of resignation. We are emotional about our horses and are desperate to want them to do it because they 'love' us, but it isn't until a horse realizes the positives that come with good behaviour that they accept it and then revel in it.

I remember when I wanted to start going out with my mates in the evening, my mum said I could but she gave me a curfew time. Her deal was that if I was ever late, she would just stop me from going out. I resented this but knew that she always stuck by her guns, so I was good about coming in on time. Eventually my curfew time got later and later as my mother trusted me to do the right thing.

HOW TO ... DESENSITIZE IN A CONTROLLED ENVIRONMENT

I had a client that sent me a three-year-old coloured cob to back. He was a lovely chap and his owner (let's call him Jack) had only been around horses for the three years that he had owned his youngster. Jack wanted to do everything right by this horse. He made the decision to keep him as naturally as possible in every sense of the word, so the horse lived out 24/7 and was kept barefoot. Jack bought him a treeless saddle, went on some natural horsemanship courses and sent him to me to be backed.

I rent boxes on a shared yard and I don't have much turnout. I am also a bit adverse to turning clients' horses out as I once had one jump out of a field and seriously injure himself.

Jack knew this at least three months before he dropped off his horse, but hadn't made any effort to get his youngster used to a stable. Well that's slightly untrue, he said he tried once or twice but the youngster didn't like it. So this poor horse was driven miles, put in a stable and then was expected to cope – of course, he was in shock for the first few days.

Although I am all for horses living out if that's what suits them, I still believe that all horses should be taught to go into a stable so that in those unexpected instances where an injury or something dictates box rest, the horse isn't stressed by the fact.

After the initial few days of shock, the cob started to get up to all sorts of mischief: he ripped the automatic waterer off the wall, flooding his own and the next door stable, and he ate, played and chewed everything in sight.

I told Jack about all his horse's escapades when he came to visit. He accepted that it was probably his fault, as to desensitize his youngster he gave him loads of 'toys' to play with in the field. That sounds great, but it taught him to respect nothing and that everything is there for his amusement, even when he is chewing his rugs and eating the saddle. Horses in the wild don't need things to amuse them; they simply eat, sleep and move around for water and new pasture. The need to give them toys is a human response, often generated by guilt in the knowledge that the lifestyle and environment we are providing is not all it should be. If you feel your youngster is getting bored, then work him, but in a controlled environment where he doesn't learn that anything is fair game. Luckily both horse and handler are now back on the right path and enjoying their time together.

Desensitization exercises

Training stick and horseman's string

If I wasn't going to show my youngster, I would split these exercises and complete them over a year by doing a small chunk over a few days and then turning the youngster away for a few months. Every now and again I would bring him back in, do a bit more and add to the schooling sessions.

However, Wonky's owner wants to show him so I need to make sure that when he goes to a show he is safe, well-educated and can perform to his maximum in the ring without feeling stressed.

I start this exercise by introducing Wonky, an eight-month-old weanling, to the equipment. Although Wonky has been handled and has travelled by trailer, he does it all unwillingly. If you put your hand on his bum, he kicks out, he doesn't like his ears being touched and is generally a domineering young man. There is absolutely nothing wrong with this, in his world that is normal colt-like behaviour and he has asserted himself as the leader in his relationship with his owner, but he is in a domesticated situation and we need him to behave in a more acceptable way.

1 I start by using my training stick and horseman's string. To begin with I keep the horseman's string close to the stick and just rub the stick over Wonky's body. Wonky's lip shape and eye tells me that he is not happy with this, but he isn't stressed and is coping with it.

2 As we all do, I have made a mistake here. As I moved the stick towards Wonky, the string came loose and fell between his ears, and he has had a huge reaction to this. This tells me a lot about Wonky: for him to have such a reaction to a bit of string between his ears shows that he could be a problem to bridle and to back, and as he gets older, more things will be used as an excuse for bad behaviour. His owner confirmed that he hates his ears and neck being touched, which is a problem as he needs to be bridled and plaited for showing.

Because Wonky is headshy, using my hand to desensitize the area will bring me too close to him and right in the line of fire. The length of the training stick means I can get to the area without being head butted and railroaded. If, like me, you do make a mistake, don't worry about it – remain calm, put it down to experience and keep going.

3 This is where Wonky is becoming resigned to the fact that the stick isn't going to eat him and that he should give it a chance. He's not jumping away from the stick but his body is leaning away from me and his eye is watching me.

4 This picture was taken about 90 seconds and 20 repetitions later, where he is now starting to accept. This is when I can start to think about moving on to the next stage. Wonky's whole demeanour has changed and he has started to blink, meaning that he is starting to think.

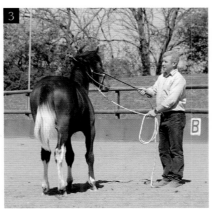

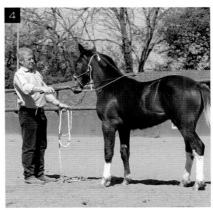

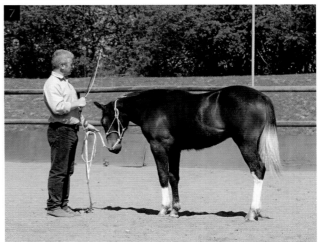

5 The next stage is to pass the stick and string over Wonky's head and body, to stimulate him above and behind the eye and to help him to lower his head and go under things. This exercise helps in lots of areas, such as headshy horses, loading (horses understand to lower their head when entering a trailer) as well as accepting a rider sitting above their eye line. In this picture Wonky has adopted the 'giraffe neck' pose and is very wary of anything that is higher than his eye line. It is imperative if you have a horse that has a problem with this that you deal with it before you consider sitting on him.

6 I keep repeating this exercise until Wonky lowers his head as soon as he sees the stick coming towards him. Again notice how his demeanour changes and he becomes very chilled out and relaxed.

7 Wonky now is very relaxed – he has really lowered his head and is even thinking about playing with the clip. I feel I can now move on to the next stage.

8 I use the string to move around his body. This exercise will show up a number of things and, as the next picture reveals, Wonky is not keen on anything on his behind.

9 What this reaction shows me is that Wonky would have had an issue with long-lines. Now I know this I can work on it before the time comes. If I don't, then I could have a potentially dangerous situation when it comes to long-lining. If you are lucky enough to have a round pen, the result wouldn't be so bad as your youngster will run around the pen. If you are backing in an open space, you could have an accident. I desensitize Wonky to this by repetition until he accepts that the string isn't going to kill him. Later when he is older and more mature physically, I will have other things I do to help with long-lining and acceptance of the lines.

Next I am going to use a plastic bag, which is an audible and visual stimulus. Again we don't want to make horses automatons but we do need to get them to control their fear and panic when they hear something that tells every cell of their being to run away.

10 I start with a small plastic bag scrunched up in my hand. This is ideal as at this stage the horse can't see the bag but he can hear it. The idea here is not to rub them with it but to pat them, so I put the bag on and lift off all over their body until he starts to relax into it – this is a form of 'advance and retreat' training, or pressure and release except that the pressure is emotional. Depending on the horse, this could take a couple of minutes or half an hour, but it is key to keep going until you start to get acceptance. You may have to move your feet initially so that you can continue. Don't be too hard on the horse about standing still – it is acceptable for them to want to walk around, and they will stand eventually when they are truly accepting.

11 Wonky here is resigned to the bag, but not totally accepting of it. His head is tilted and too high, but at least he is not running over me.

12 The rope here is totally slack and although his ears are back they are showing me that he is paying attention to what is going on behind him. It's not a sign of grumpiness.

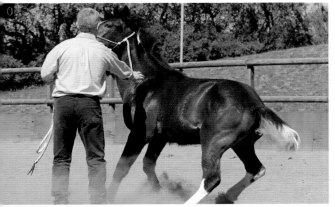

13 This is a really good picture as it is the first time that he has licked and chewed since I started this work with the bag, so he is starting to think about what is happening and realizing that the bag isn't going to eat him. Remember to watch and listen for all the signs of acceptance.

I increased the size of the bag each time Wonky showed me he had accepted the current situation.

14 Once the horse has accepted the plastic bag, you can introduce other things. I have now gone on to a coat, which is probably a good one as I see a number of people having problems on their horses when they want to either put on or take off a rustling jacket. I started with this coat folded up and worked up to opening it out.

HANDY TIP

These exercises are also good for pre-rug training.

A bag on a stick

Passers by and other liveries on my yard often look at me as though I am barking mad when I do this exercise, maybe they are right. The next item I am going to introduce to Wonky is the bag on a stick. What this does is to break up the stimulation and divide his attention – we are going to stimulate both behind and in front of his eyeline (line of vision). Behind the eyeline helps prepare for backing and also will eventually help with traffic coming from behind. In front of the eye really helps with items coming towards him, such as traffic, and also with preparation for hacking and all the wildlife that jumps out at you.

1 A quick reminder that before you start any of this work, your youngster must be halter trained and respect your personal space (see pages 54–61) – this will prevent you from being run over.

I start by standing in front of Wonky and leaving enough space between him and me so that if he does get a fright, he can run around me and not over me. Then I put the stick with the bag out in front of me. You can see here that Wonky is mildly curious – his head is up and his body is leaning slightly back – but I know he is not really worried as his ears are pricked.

2 With the bag and initially standing still, I bring the stick either side, up above my head and then down to the side on each side. I then repeat when we are on the move.

3 Right eye stimulation.

4 Imitating an animal jumping up out of the undergrowth.

5 As I am walking I have the bag out in front of me, where Wonky can't see it. I then flick it from one side to the other.

6 Don't just take it from side to side at right angles but flick it out low or high – use your imagination. Wonky is becoming so cool about it all.

7 Everything here is perfect: Wonky's posture and the slack in the rope. We have stimulated in front and behind the eye. I now turn and face him.

8 I get Wonky to make the bag yield from him rather than him yield from the bag. In effect Wonky is pushing the bag. This makes him brave and is a really good confidence giver to horses that are a bit windy and spooky – it gives them courage.

9 I am running backwards and Wonky is really determined to chase it – it's a bit of fun and he seems to enjoy it.

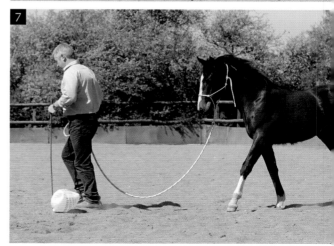

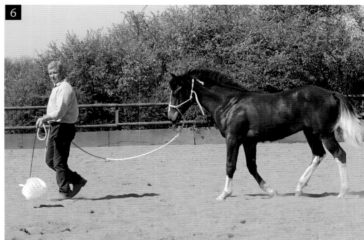

6 MONTHS–3 YEARS

Avoiding the terrible twos

It is at this time that young horses go through huge changes and can often turn into 'teenagers' over night.

This is why I like to establish ground rules before my youngsters turn two – I was never any good at wrestling at school and I really don't want to have to start now with an opponent that is ten times stronger than I am.

By putting the basics in place, I find that I get less attitude than with horses that don't have any boundaries established, and when they do think they might like to have a bit of attitude, I am able to manage it.

This period generally runs from about the age of 18 months to two and half years. It can vary, but as a rule it is during this time frame that you can expect the worst behaviour and where your youngster will challenge you the most. This is the time when halter training and the establishment of your personal space are really important.

TIPS FOR AVOIDING THE TERRIBLE TWOS

- Go over what your youngster already knows rather than try teach him anything new it is the new things what will cause the most arguments during training.
- Keep the sessions short and don't over do it – their attention span will be short, and it will save you all sorts of falling out. Only repeat work for a maximum of three days back to back and then turn them out again for a month or more.
- If you are struggling to understand how this works, then think back to being a teenager – it's an awful time, hormones are raging and nobody can do the right thing and you probably often felt that you couldn't do the right thing.

Remember, if a horse had a good grounding before the hormones kicked in, it won't be long before he goes back to being a normal horse again. Kids that really end up in trouble during their teens are often the ones that didn't have a good situation before it started. I read a study a few years ago about teenagers and the feelings that they go through. The one point that stood out the most for me was the teenagers who said it was the lack of discipline and direction that caused them to go off the rails and also the lack of direction and discipline that made it difficult for them to integrate back into society when their peers were getting back to normal.

It will be normal for your youngster to have the odd temper tantrum. The key is to work through it quietly. However, I have found that it is definitely easier to stick with what they know between the ages of 18 to 30 months

Preparing for the farrier

Feet for me are one of the 'must dos' because once you can handle a horse's feet, you will have a horse that is easier to handle all round, and the earlier you start the better. It is definitely one of those areas where you will see huge positive knock-on effects – if you get it right, you'll get a lot more than just a horse that is happy to have its feet handled.

The primary need to handle a horse's feet is for welfare, regardless of how you decide to shoe or not to shoe your horse. Remember it is not your farrier's job to train your horse to have his feet handled, it is yours!

The first step is to get your horse comfortable with having his feet handled as this is necessary for day-to-day care and picking out.

One of the biggest mistakes I have found is the lack of preparation for the farrier and it is a genuine oversight rather than something people are doing wrong. Most young horses will have had their feet picked out long before the first visit from the farrier, but very few will have had their feet and legs pulled into or held into the correct position for trimming or shoeing.

What I mean is that when we pick out a foot, we pick it up and hold it with one hand and pick it out with the other, keeping the foot close to the ground. When the farrier handles the feet, he will put the horse's front feet between his legs and the hind feet in his lap when removing the shoes and pull the leg up and forward when he is doing the clenches or finishing off. All these positions are different to day-to-day handling and are much higher off the ground.

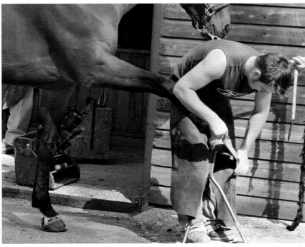

Look at how a farrier picks up your horse's feet and where he puts them

A good thing to do with your youngster is to start putting his feet in the same positions as the farrier does so that when the day arrives he doesn't think the difference is that big and panic. It's the lack of clarity in these situations that can cause confusion and upset with young horses.

If you have a horse that is nervous of the farrier, ask the farrier nicely if he would lend you an old apron or sweatshirt that you can wear when you are training your youngster. On a daily basis, using the repetitions I have talked about, practise holding your youngster's feet as a farrier would. If you want to take this exercise a step further, you could get something safe but made of metal and tap at his feet, not hard but just in a rhythm that he can get used to.

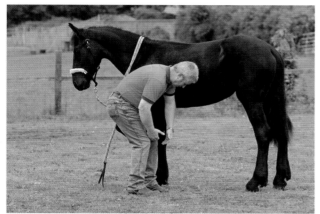

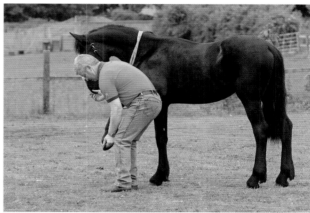

Once you have thought about the way a farrier picks up a horse's feet, try to use this information when you are training your youngster to meet the farrier

Bathing

Being able to bath your youngster isn't just about him looking good and keeping clean, it is also about being able to treat him for cuts and any possible skin conditions and to hose any swellings.

As I keep saying, to tackle these situations your horse needs to be well established in his halter training so that both of you can be kept safe. I start by using a bucket of warm water and a sponge; this will lessen the shock to the horse and by using a sponge I can move around with my youngster as he wanders about, which is normal at the start. About 90 per cent of youngsters will wander around, and the other 10 per cent will want to run into or over you, which is when the halter training and the respect of personal space is important.

Once I know he is happy, I repeat the exercise using cold water and only when he has accepted this will I move on to a cold water hose.

This is generally where I see most people that have horses that don't like hoses make mistakes. The owners take their horse to the hosepipe, then pull the hose out and turn it on. The water splurts out in fits and starts making a hissing sound, and then the owner wonders why the horse is freaked out and why they can't get him near the hose.

I would suggest that before you take your horse to the wash area, you put the hose out and run the water through it so that all the spluttering and gurgling has stopped. You can turn the hose off whilst you collect your horse so as not to waste water but at least it is all set up ready to go.

Unfortunately, on the yard shown here there was only a short hose. We got round this situation because the horse was halter trained, but it would have been better to have had a longer hose.

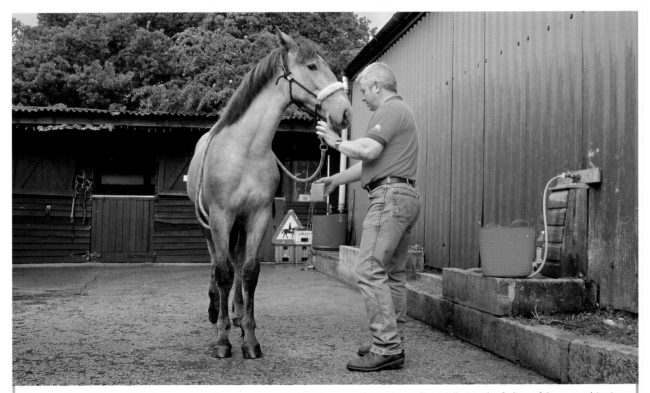

Keep wetting the horse with the sponge and warm water until he is happy and standing still; initially it is the feeling of the water dripping down the leg that makes the horse want to wander about

When doing exercises like this, I always work from front feet to back feet, from the nearside to the offside and from the foot working up the leg. All the horses that I have worked with over the years, whether they have a problem with the hosepipe or not, have responded to this introduction of water really well.

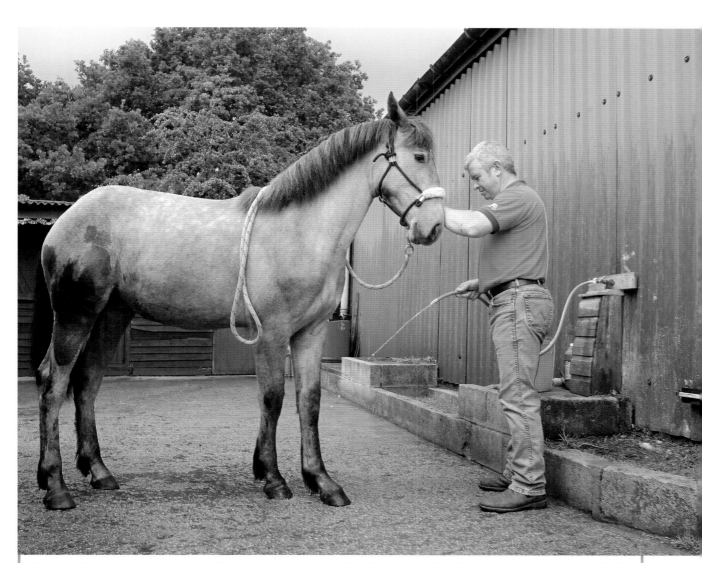

Now that this youngster can be washed off it means that he is prepared for all eventualities. We all hope that we don't need to deal with cut legs that may need washing off and stitching, but unfortunately it's a fact of owning horses. Being prepared for all eventualities is the key to good horse management

Clipping

Horses that don't like being clipped are some of the most regular calls I get. For this reason I introduce clipping early because if it goes wrong, it has the potential to go very wrong.

In this session I am not looking to actually clip Silverson's Samara, a Spanish Norman filly, but just to introduce her to the clippers and the sensation. If this is repeated for a few days every couple of months, by the time she comes to be clipped she won't notice what is happening as she will be so used to the clippers and the feel of them against her body.

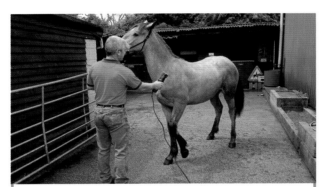

1 By walking directly towards Samara with the clippers, I have made her feel quite threatened. Look at her eyes and ears – everything about them tells you she is thinking backwards. She is looking for an escape route.

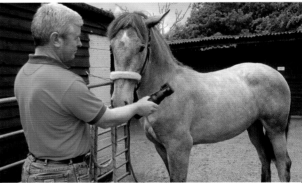

3 As these two pictures show, allowing Samara to feel the vibrations quickly turns her from being very wary to being very quizzical. The great part about showing things to youngsters is that their speed of learning is amazing.

2 When first introducing the clippers, I stand to the side of the horse and let her explore them. At this stage I wouldn't have them turned on. Once she has become more curious, I turn them on and let her feel the vibrations through my body. This does two things: she is given a sense of the vibrations in a diluted form and it allows her to become used to the noise of the clippers.

SAFETY FIRST

Remember to keep yourself safe at all times. If you know your horse doesn't like clippers, get a cordless pair and work on a safe surface such as a menage.

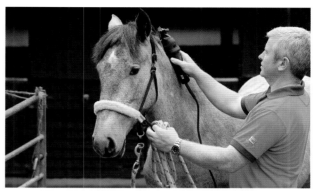

5 Once I can see she is happy with all areas of her body, I move on to the head and ears.

4 Once I see that the youngster is happy with the situation, I move the clippers to the body, normally to the shoulder as I find it's the safest place to start. Don't forget, I am not looking to actually clip any hair at this stage. Once she is happy with the neck area, I move the clippers all over her body. See how relaxed she has become; her eye and ear are very soft, and she is no longer looking for a way out.

If you do this from a very young age, by the time your youngster comes to be clipped it will all fall into place and you won't get any bad reactions. Don't leave things to chance, and think that because you've done it once it will still be ok, do this at regular intervals throughout their young lives.

Another great way of introducing clippers, or at least their sensation, is through a massage machine. I use these regularly on my own horses and they all love being clipped and totally chill out.

If your horse really doesn't like the clippers, it is important to reward positive and not negative behaviour. When your horse is accepting the clippers or hand-held massager, then you can remove it. If your horse is moving about, try to keep the clippers on your horse – you may have to move around a bit yourself. As soon as he settles, take away the clippers or massager to reward the try. It is easy to inadvertently train your horse to not accept the clippers.

Injections

One of the most dangerous situations I have witnessed was a vet trying to inject a horse that didn't like needles. It really made me think about how you would retrain a horse to accept a needle. Being a needle-shy person myself, I had every sympathy with the horse.

Good groundwork is going to be key here as you really do need your horse to be respectful of your personal space. If he does have issues with needles, this is the one factor that will cause him to want to run over the top of you.

The tools you will need are:
- A thick elastic band
- A large plastic syringe
- Carrots or some form of treat
- Last but not least, patience!

This is the only exercise I do that involves treats. When the horse feels the sting/pain of the needle, I give him a treat to distract him from the sting. Horses can't think about two things at once, which is why it works so well and why I would use treats in this instance.

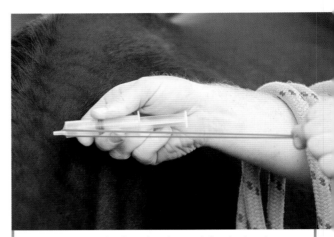

I start by hooking the elastic band around the plastic syringe and holding it close to the skin. I pull the elastic band back until it is quite tight and let go. This will sting the horse probably a bit more than an injection would, so it's straight after this moment that I give the horse the treat to take his mind off the sting. I keep repeating this and after each time I give the horse a treat. Eventually he will start to look for the treat, which will relax him. A relaxed muscle is far less painful than a tense one

INTRODUCING SOMETHING NEW

As mentioned earlier, when I introduce something that has the potential to cause a reaction, I always do this after a period of work. With a youngster I don't mean schooling work but something that has caused him to think and use the more analytical side of his brain.

Make the treat an apple or carrot. I tend not to use pony nuts as they aren't quite as tempting

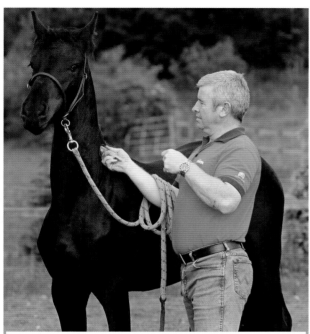

Look at the position of this youngster's head – he is watching my every move and is very wary

Keep up this training until the vet visits and make sure you are there with your treat. You will find that once the horse is coping with injections, you can reduce the treats if you want to.

Although this process originally came about because of horses that had become needle shy, I now practise this on youngsters so that the problem doesn't arise in the first place. It's all back to preparation – why wait until it's all gone wrong?

Just as I was finishing this book our children's pony had a terrible accident that meant he had to be injected every day for three weeks. I used the above method, even though he wasn't a problem, to prevent the situation becoming one. Every day the vet calls me, he can't believe what an amazing chap this pony is – not once has he gone to the back of his box when it comes to that time of day.

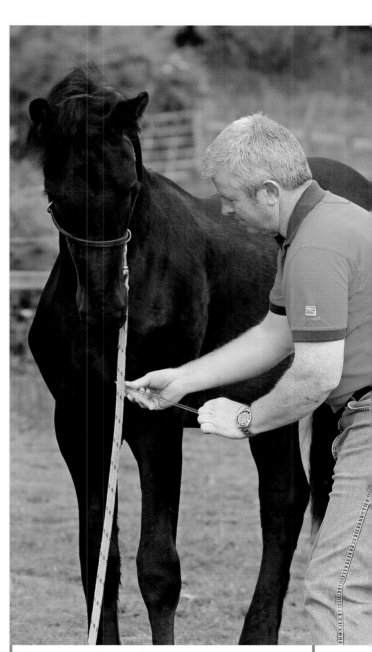

The same horse after I have been giving him treats. He has started to ignore the injection and to look for the reward. I would repeat this process on every part of the horse's body that has the potential to be injected

6 MONTHS–3 YEARS

Preparing for loading

If you think about what a horse has to go through to go into either a horsebox or a trailer and apply those concepts to your early training, your horse will find the whole process much less stressful. Although the following exercises are good for young horses, you can still use them with older horses.

Horses are pre-conditioned at birth not to walk over strange things, not to go into narrow spaces and definitely never to go down dead ends or into caves. They stay in wide open spaces so that they can see their predators and flee when necessary. It's therefore no surprise that many horses are wary of loading in the first instance.

Early loading can start well before a young horse ever sees a horsebox or trailer. I am going to split up the process into three separate areas that you need to teach the horse.

1. **Walking over and standing on lots of different surfaces.** I am going to start with a tarpaulin sheet on the ground and a large piece of ply-board. This gets the horse used to walking on and over strange surfaces.
2. **Walking through narrow spaces.** I am going to start walking him through and between objects that create a tight spot.
3. **Walking under something and lowering his head.** I ask the horse to walk under a lungeing stick.

By putting all this training in place, you can teach your horse in a safe environment how to cope with all these tasks. Only once your youngster is totally happy and calm in all of these tasks should you even consider taking him to a trailer.

Here we have Wonky again. Although he has been handled by his owner and has obviously loaded to come to us, he isn't happy about a lot of things in his training and definitely sees himself as the boss in their relationship.

First we must ensure that Wonky respects the halter and understands that we know the rules of pressure and release. Then I am going to start working on the tarpaulin.

Once you have committed yourself and turned your youngster to face the tarp, you cannot allow him to turn away from it. You must keep him facing the tarp even if that means you have to move your feet slightly – that doesn't matter as long as he continues to face the tarp

Counter movement – here I have moved my body to counter the movement

I don't mind if a youngster wants to check out and explore the tarp when I first start working with him on new tasks as long as he doesn't use it as an avoidance tactic

When he goes to run back, allow him to run to the end of the rope, but don't pull him. Maintain the level of pressure, even if you have to allow with your arm. If you have done your halter training properly, then he should give to the pressure, as seen here, and come to you

Your youngster will mess around. This is normal and you just have to be patient and remain calm – remember you are asking a lot of him. He will put one foot on then take it off again. Once he has put two feet on, position yourself to get out of the way, as shown by my body language. When he puts two feet on the tarp, it will feel strange to him, the sand under the tarp will move and 99 per cent of horses will explode forward and leap off the tarp

As shown here, horses really are predictable creatures

Keep repeating the process until he is walking calmly over the tarp – notice how low Wonky's head has become

You will need to repeat the whole process again in the opposite direction. It shouldn't take as long but you will generally get a reaction. Keep repeating again until you have your horse walking calmly over the tarp

Once you have him walking calmly over the tarp, just ask him to stand on it and chill out – give him a rub and get him used to standing quietly regardless of the situation

Finally, to complete this section, replace the tarp with a large, safe piece of wood. I wouldn't expect the reaction to be explosive – this exercise just allows the youngster to get the feel of the wood and the noise that it makes under foot. You can do some exercises such as backing him off the wood and asking him to come forward again. Also ask him to stand on the surface and stay still for quite long periods. This teaches him to chill out when asked to stand, which will be important once you start to load and travel to different places. The more you can do, the more relaxed he will become about anything you ask of him

Loading

Ideally, loading should be split up into three separate tasks: loading, staying on and putting up the ramp. Each task in its own right is a lot for a young horse, or an older horse that is a problem loader. There will always be those horses that are capable and can achieve all three areas in one day, but to be fairer this is not what I would recommend.

Loading is one of those areas that everyone dreads, but if you do your homework, it really isn't that bad. You will only run into problems if you don't do any preparation. If you have done all the other tasks set out in this book, you will be fine. This advice also applies if you have an older horse that has loading problems, it just takes a bit longer.

For loading a youngster I would use a horseman's halter and a 12 foot (3.6m) rope – this is vital because if he runs backwards, you can allow him to do so without causing either of you any harm. If you have an older horse that is refusing to load, I find that a normal halter doesn't have the same effect and the horse becomes numb to it. I would use a pressure halter, but again you would have to school him in it first so that he understands what it is all about. You will run into trouble if you put on a pressure halter and go straight to the trailer.

The hardest part about loading is that once you have succeeded for the first time, you need to unload and then reload 50 times. Initially, you may find that at some point in those 50 loads your horse will test you – do you mean what you say and are you committed to seeing it through? If your horse tests you, stick to the method, but your 50 loads start again and it's not until you have succeeded with 50 correct loads in a row that you should end the session. For the next week you must repeat this exercise everyday so that at the end of the first week you and your horse have completed 300 successful loads.

RULES OF LOADING

1. Make sure your ramp and transport are safe and don't have any sharp edges. With young horses remove the partition – that can come later.
2. Always park at least the ramp and half the transport on a safe surface, either a field or a menage. Never ever park on concrete, gravel or tarmac – this is the surest way to injure your horse. Unfortunately, loading is one of those things that can cause your horse to rear in the early stages (about one in 20 horses will go over or sit down) – if a youngster goes up on gravel, he may lose his footing and slip over, the same goes for concrete or tarmac.
3. On the day you decide to deal with loading, make sure you have all the time in the world.
4. Your horse needs a 100 per cent understanding of pressure and release.
5. Once you have presented your horse to the trailer there is no going back – you must never turn him away from the ramp until he has loaded a number of times.
6. Once you horse enters the trailer, *no matter what*, you must *never* put any form of pressure on him.
7. If you have a trailer with a front unload, *do not* open it – only use the rear ramp.
8. Do not walk your youngster through the trailer – he must learn to stand in it not walk through it.
9. Do not use titbits to encourage, only praise for a job well done.
10. Do not accept a half job, if half a hoof is still on the ramp the job is *not* done.

Once your youngster is going on without hesitation, you can think about closing him in. When you first do this, just have him stand in the trailer without going anywhere. This is so important – you have no idea how many people call to say that their loading issue is the time between the ramp going up and the car driving away. Horses have climbed over the breast bar, gone under the breast bar, generally been a pain in the bum jumping up and down and kicking the trailer – the list goes on.

If you find that your youngster is panicked about the ramp, then you will need to call in two helpers and get yourself a large blanket that covers the area where the ramp goes. Stand inside the trailer with your horse on a long rope, get your friends to take the blanket and stand either side of trailer but *never ever* behind the trailer – I have seen some bad accidents where the horse has come out at a million miles an hour and trampled the helpers. Quietly get your friends to hold the blanket up to the trailer like a ramp. They should hold the blanket at each corner and position themselves so that they can mimic the ramp going up. If your horse feels the need to run out, they can drop the blanket and your horse won't be injured. Again don't put any pressure on your horse until his head is clear of the trailer, then invite him back in. Repeat this exercise until your youngster is happy to stay in with the blanket up for a good few minutes. Only then try the ramp.

Make your youngster's first journey about 30 minutes or more. If you are near to a motorway or dual carriage way, then a good trip on either one of those is much better than short jerky trips that don't allow the youngster to settle into travelling. Two to three repetitions in one day is better than stringing this out over weeks or months.

Having a horse that doesn't load is a nightmare – not necessarily because you can't get to an event but also in an emergency. Making the effort to ensure that your horse will load and be comfortable is time well spent

HOW TO ... LOAD

1 Once you are set up, you must first spend five or ten minutes doing some halter work away from the trailer so that your youngster is in the right frame of mind for work. When he is responding well to the work, you can take him to the trailer. Remember that once you have presented him there is no turning away. If you do, your horse will become more and more committed to not going on. With a young horse I allow him to check out the ramp, but once he has had a good sniff that is it. This is an exercise in loading not ramp sniffing, and he will use it as a tactic to avoid going in the trailer. Praise every forward movement with a release of the rope.

2 Take up the rope and with only a small amount of pressure, ask him to step forward onto the ramp. This is generally ok – the problem normally comes when he has his two front feet on the ramp and doesn't know how to get his back feet on as well.

3 This is the typical stance of both a youngster and an older horse when he gets stuck. Allow some thinking time but watch to make sure he hasn't zoned out and shut down – you'll know this because there won't be any eye movement.

If he has zoned out and grown roots, you need to maintain the pressure on the rope and quietly move his head from side to side. By doing this you are annoying him and putting him under pressure, and he cannot zone out on you. One of two things will happen: he will either walk forward or run backwards. If the latter occurs, follow with the rope and don't tighten your hand on the rope until he is off the ramp. Then ask him to come forward again and repeat the exercise.

4 Hopefully, he will come forward, even if it is by a small step. Note in this picture that the horse has raised his back foot and is moving forward so I have released the pressure on his halter.

5 As he gets nearer the entrance, he starts to raise his head. Be careful at this point that he doesn't go up and hit his head. Remain quietly calm and purposeful and praise every forward thought – watch for him swaying his body towards you.

6 Now he has all four feet on the ramp and has got stuck. Although I can't be seen here, I am maintaining the pressure on the rope and quietly moving from side to side. (Notice how many times I use the word 'quietly'. That is because this isn't about dragging them about and pulling their heads off.)

7 Bingo! He decides to walk in, but his back legs are still on the ramp. This

is where you have to be really subtle. You need to ask him to step forward but you don't want to put so much pressure on that he throws his head up and hits it on the roof. If he goes to run out backwards, let him go and do not tighten your grip on the rope until he is off the ramp. Once he has stopped, do not turn him away but ask him to come forward once again.

8 Because he has got really stuck and I don't want to cause him to bang his head, I reverse him off and start again. It is worth going back a step rather than causing a situation that will take a long time to reverse.

9 Now he is trying avoidance tactics, but it his responsibility to sort himself out not yours. Don't be tempted to take him off the ramp, stand your ground and ask him nicely to come forward into the trailer.

10 He has decided it is far easier to go in than to mess about.

11 Hurray! He is in – back feet and all! Now it is vital that you allow him to stand in the trailer quietly to learn that you don't load and then reverse straight out. This is so important if you have to load your horse on your own. A horse that will stand whilst you sort things out is worth his weight in gold. Only when they can stand quietly and allow you to do all that is necessary would you put the back up.

6 MONTHS–3 YEARS

Preparing for a bridle

Although this exercise is a great way of getting a young horse used to the process of putting a bridle on, it is also how I would help a horse that had bridling issues or was generally headshy.

There are undoubtedly thousands of horses that have no issues with the bridle and the bit – you can walk up to them and pop it straight on with little or no effort at all. The ones that do object, however, can do so in a big way – there is nothing pleasant about having a bridle slung round your head when trying to get it on a horse that is bigger and stronger than you.

The following process is great for young and older horses. With young horses this is how I would start and with older horses this is where I would start the re-training process. It will probably look mighty strange as there won't be a bridle in sight at the start.

With young horses the training is all about preparing them for feelings and sensations so that something becomes familiar. Then when the day comes for you to introduce them to the end result, it becomes a natural progression.

You can start this preparation as young as three days old, or anytime after that. For me, the younger you start to show them something, the easier it becomes for them to accept it.

If you think about putting on a bridle and break it up into small pieces, there are three main elements: first, the horse needs to open his mouth; second, you move the bridle up their face; and finally, it goes over the ears. So this is what we are going to show the horse.

HOW TO ... PREPARE FOR A BRIDLE

I start with my finger, you could use a small blunt piece of wood shaped like a pencil, if you don't want to use your finger. I place my finger inside the side of the horse's mouth. I am aiming for him to get used to the fact that finger in the mouth means open it for the bit – it becomes a conditioned response. When I do come to use a bit, I will use a rubber or plastic one so it doesn't bang his teeth and give him a shock. Once he is taking the bit readily, I move on to a sweet iron bit.

Once I have done that, I am going to move my hand up his face and over the eye and ear in a sweeping fashion to simulate the bridle going up and over his ears.

I repeat this on both sides, which forms a pattern of behaviour in his mind: something in my mouth, hand goes up and over my face and ears. The fact that you'll eventually have a bridle in your hand will have no consequences as you have prepared him for that day.

If you are looking for activities, there are lots you can do before the day arrives for his first ever bridle. Use your imagination – as long as you don't frighten your horse you'll be fine. Here I have used a piece of rope to take the place of the bridle at this young age – it's soft so it can't hurt even if you don't get it right the first few times.

Why do some horses object to the bit?

As I said at the beginning, I also use this method for horses that have started to refuse their bridle, but there are often reasons why horses start to object, so look at the following first.

Are your horse's teeth too sharp? You can check this yourself. If you stand on your horse's near side, using your left hand, place it on your horse's nose and put your left thumb in your horse's mouth along the side – don't go putting your thumb or hand directly into his mouth or you'll get bitten. Rub your thumb up towards the back of the mouth along the teeth and you will be able to feel any sharp edges. This will cause a particular problem if your horse has a fleshy inside cheek.

Next check your horse's tongue. One of my horses has a really fleshy tongue, and putting a fat bit in his mouth would cause him a lot of discomfort as the pressure of the bit on his tongue would be too much. Whereas many people automatically assume that a fat bit is kinder, he needs a really thin bit to make him comfortable (actually he prefers no bit but as I compete him that isn't an option for some elements).

Lastly, if your horse has suddenly become headshy, have the vet check for ear mites. These are little critters that get overlooked and simple drops will get rid of them.

Circling work

Circling work is now a huge part of my training regime, and I have found that it is rather like dropping a stone into a pond – the ripples will reach every shore. The effects of circling work touch every single aspect of my training, whether in a large or small way.

When training any horse for any job, a circle will always play a part in developing the horse's way of going no matter what system of training is used. With this in mind, I felt I had to come up with a way of working with a horse on a circle that was interesting to all parties. I don't know about you but I have always found lungeing mind-numbingly boring, and if I do, then you can be sure a horse does. I have noticed that after three times around a circle a horse switches off, so I have to either change direction or change pace to keep the horse truly focused on me as the handler.

As with everything I do, I start off very obvious and work towards the subtle. To me, there are two main elements to doing circling work: first, to gain control of the quarters and second, to gain control of the shoulders.

I always start with the quarters, as these are the horse's engine and being able to move them around gives greater control without force. When I say control, I mean the ability to 'disengage' them, and this then not only gives me the tool to stop bucking and bolting but also on a more positive note it gives better engagement, flexion and dexterity. Not bad for one small exercise.

The next thing is to be able to move the shoulders out onto a circle away from you. By having control of the shoulders I am able to deal with rearing, spinning and spooking before it happens. It also gives me better control of the front of the horse as I am able to lift the shoulders to get the horse off his forehand and on to his quarters. The in-between element is that it teaches the horse the discipline of the circle. This now enables me to interact with the horse and to have the left side of his brain working more than the right, which ultimately leads to a much safer horse, which means having more fun.

Circling

You can start this exercise with just a halter and 12 foot (3.6m) rope. I prefer to use one with a tassel as it can be a tactile cue if I need one.

Look at your horse and draw an imaginary driving line around his middle just behind the withers. This gives you two areas to think about: the shoulders, which are in front of the driving line, and the quarters, which are behind.

Stand with your shoulder in line with your driving line. Look at your horse's quarters and spin your rope at the quarters – do not spin it like a mad thing, but use a nice rhythm, spinning it over arm not under arm (if you keep beating yourself with the rope, your elbow is probably too close to your body, so move your elbow out and you should be ok). If your horse doesn't respond, up the tempo of your spin; if he still ignores you, then let the tassel touch his quarters on each rotation (but don't beat him with it). If he still ignores you, smack the ground with your rope causing an audible and a visual stimulus.

You are looking for your horse to move his quarters away from you by stepping the hind leg nearest you through and under. This needs to be repeated on both sides to keep increasing your horse's dexterity and flexion.

When sending your horse away from you through his shoulder, first stand facing your horse at about 3 foot (1m) away. Hold your left hand out at shoulder height and with the right hand spin the rope towards the head, neck and shoulder. This will have the effect of driving your horse out on to the circle through his shoulder.

Repeat this exercise on both sides until your horse starts to move away before you spin the rope.

To stop your horse circling around you, you need to put pressure on his quarters. This is putting into practice what you have already taught him. What will happen is that he will step through from behind, move his quarters out and turn to face you.

Whilst your horse is on the circle going to the left, run your left hand down the rope taking a feel on his head, and at the same time spin the end of the rope at this quarters. Don't get upset if it takes a few goes for him to understand – you are asking a lot of him to think whilst on the move.

When he does understand and turns to face you, it is important that you don't let him creep into your personal space. We have already taught him to stand in his own space, so use those techniques.

Once you have mastered the rope circling, you can use it as part of your programme with a saddle on.

ARE YOU A VISUAL LEARNER?

Personally, I am a very visual learner and struggle to understand some things that are written down, and, interestingly, I was receiving a number of calls about this in relation to the groundwork. I have now made a DVD that shows all the groundwork I use to help visual learners. I have used horses and their owners to show the mistakes that can be made and how to correct them, and it also covers long-lining. If you are interested, further details can be found at www.richard-maxwell.com.

Questions and answers

Q Max, I need your help. My yearling filly just refuses to trot when I lead her in hand. I have done pressure and release to get her to lead in hand and she is now perfect in walk. The problem begins when I start to try for a trot. She just grinds to a halt and looks at me like I am an alien. She won't even trot towards home or her feed bucket. I have got a show in three weeks so need to get her trotting.

A I'd use a 12 foot (3.6m) rope, go to the very end of it and ask her to trot on, positioning yourself at least 10–12 foot (3–3.6m) away from her, as this will give her enough visual room to move into. Once the penny has started to drop about moving her feet at the same time as you, start to make the length of the rope less and less by about 1 foot (0.3m) at a time until she is trotting next to your shoulder. The common problem with getting babies to trot up is that most people want the end result straightaway, but it needs to be back to breaking things down and aiming for the end result. Again, see pages 54–61 for halter training and pages 78–9 for the example of Gwin, a Fresian mare, that had this problem.

My final word would be to say that I wouldn't take any horse to a show unless I knew they were 100 per cent respectful of their halter and you.

A Teaching a youngster to turn right is actually one of those things that often gets neglected in the early stages. It feels very awkward and like most things that feel awkward it is very important. Please don't ignore this one as when it is done well, it will have a positive effect on the horse's life.

To start with you need to be very obvious when you ask for that turn. Once the horse has got the hang of it, you can go back to being very subtle.

The first thing I do is to guide the youngster's face away to the right with an open hand and the shoulders should follow the direction of the nose. Once he is moving to the right with the open hand, you can start to reduce the visual of the hand to a finger and then eventually to your body.

As I make the right turn, I hold my hand up to guide the nose and turn my own body into the youngster's neck. In this picture the youngster has put his head up, but as he starts to get what I would like, he will keep his head low

The youngster now tips his nose in the direction that I want to go. Keep practising and the turns will become easier. Your youngster will start to watch your body movements and will make sure that he keeps out of your way

Questions and answers

Q I am having very serious problems with our youngster rearing in the ring, striking out at me and today he came down on my, thankfully protected, head. He started doing this at home about a month or so ago, but we got on top of that really quickly. Now he just does it in the ring when on the move, but stands as good as gold in the line up.

A It is exactly this for this reason that I use a 12 foot (3.6m) rope. Make sure when you are leading him that you leave enough rope between you and him so that when he goes up he doesn't suck you underneath him. Then when he is on his hind feet, it is important that he is disciplined at that point. You can do this by shaking the rope at him quite vigorously, but as soon as his feet are back on the floor you must rub and praise him. I know this is hard but it is important that he knows that being up is not a good place to be and having all four feet on the ground is the right place.

Q Could you give me some advice about worming my foal?

A Worming is one of those events that every horse has to go through and yet another one of those subjects that is very much debated. Below is a worming programme and some recommendations I found on an independent website regarding worming.

- De-worm the mare just before foaling to minimize the contamination of the new foal's environment.
- Start worming the foal at four to six weeks old. Repeat every four weeks until six months old and then follow an adult worming programme.
- It is vital that foals are wormed as they are susceptible to massive infestations of roundworms, which may physically block the intestines, and threadworms, which can cause diarrhoea and unthriftness.
- Roundworms are passed from foal to foal, so if possible don't graze foals on pasture that was grazed by foals and yearlings the year before.

As you can see from these recommendations, you need to get yourself organized with regards to worming. If your youngster objects to the worming process, you can start with him as early as three days old by using an empty plastic syringe full of something tasty such as apple puree. Once you have started to worm for real, you can follow up the treatment with a tube of apple puree.

I use exactly the same process to introduce a horse to a bit that I do when I want to get a youngster used to worming, but I would move onto a plastic syringe, and if needed you can fill it with something tasty such as apple puree. Start by letting your foal investigate the object and then move onto putting it in their mouth, by using a plastic syringe filled with something you will get their curiosity. Once you have to start worming for real you can always follow it with an apple or something similar

Q I am having trouble getting my youngster to stand at the mounting block, he keeps moving off before I want him to.

A Being still is not something that comes naturally to horses of any age, especially youngsters. I have also seen many clients that have lost their confidence because of an incident at the mounting block, so it is important to invest the time at an early age.

Ideally, if you have an unbacked youngster, practise taking them to the mounting block and ask them to stand. Every time they move away, put them back in the spot that you want, and keep building on this. Once your youngster is standing, then start walking up the mounting block so that they get used to you being above them. If it will help you to feel more comfortable, then ask a friend to help you.

However, as your youngster is already backed, you are going to have to use a bit of reverse psychology and get him to think that it's the best and easiest place to be. There are a couple of things that you can try:

1. Every time you are working in the school, always come to rest by the mounting block.
2. Take the mounting block into the middle of the school and do circling work around it. Always bring your horse back to the mounting block to rest, and if he wants to move away from it, then send him back to work until he realizes that standing quietly is easier than being sent away. A horse that doesn't stand still will only become more fidgety if made to stand still. Some people tell me that this technique doesn't work for their horse, whereas I haven't met a horse that it doesn't work for. What I have found though is that many horse owners give up too soon.

By giving Moss all the time she needed for her training, mounting never became an issue – it was just another task she did on a daily basis without thinking about it

This is the first time that Moss's owner has got on Moss at a mounting block. Moss has been so well trained that it doesn't enter her head to move off until she is asked

PART 4

Backing and riding on

It is significant that in an entire book on training young horses, the section about backing and riding the horse for the first time takes up only the very last quarter. For me, this is an accurate reflection of its importance.

I think that people get unnecessarily stressed about the moment a horse is sat on for the first time, and this is often communicated to the animal on the one day when he needs to be as calm and accepting as possible.

A QUICK CHECKLIST

Hopefully you will have in place everything outlined below. If you don't it's never too late to start. Before working on the techniques in this part, read through the checklist below, you can also use these exercises to correct unwanted behaviour.

1. Does he accept being bathed?
2. Is he prepared for his first clipping?
3. Does he load?
4. Does he tie up?
5. Is his advanced halter training completed?
6. Is he ready for the farrier?
7. Is he prepared for his first bridle?
8. Does he need further desensitization exercises?

If your answer to some of these questions is 'no', you can go back and do some further work on these elements before starting to back your youngster.

The first saddle

The saddle can be introduced well before you decide to back your youngster. I like to introduce it fairly early on and then continue with groundwork and long-lining or ride and lead with the tack on.

The traditional way of backing horses uses a roller. However, I found that even having introduced a roller, I might still get a reaction to the saddle, whereas once a horse is used to the saddle, a roller is never an issue.

Often after the first session with the saddle when young horses are backed, they are taken back to their box for a job well done. I like to ensure that, when I come out the next day, the youngster doesn't have any backwards thoughts and is emotionally comfortable about what I ask.

I am looking for 50 successful repetitions in a row. Once the initial introduction is complete and the youngster is comfortable wearing the saddle, going in all directions and in all three paces, I will undo the girth, lift the saddle off, put it back on, do the girth up and ask him to go out on a circle for one turn in both directions and then repeat this process 50 times. It may take an hour but it will be time well spent.

I would repeat this over the next five days so that in his first week he will have had 250 positive experiences of the saddle – more than some ridden horses get in a year.

This exercise is excellent for horses that struggle with the saddle as it cancels out the number of negative experiences and builds up the number of good.

HOW TO ... INTRODUCE THE FIRST SADDLE

This is Hermione. I start the session by introducing the saddle cloth. As I did with the plastic bag on Wonky, I rub it all over her body. This is mainly as a familiarization exercise and I will do this until she starts to ignore it and becomes relaxed. I can tell by her posture that she is OK and will be fine with the saddle

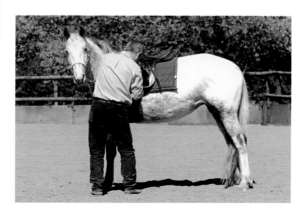

She is so chilled – her eye is really soft and I can tell that she has been well prepared for this moment

Now that she has a saddle on, I ask her to step back before asking her to move off on to a circle. When a horse hasn't worn a saddle before, the sensation is very strange and Hermione gets stuck, so I help her to move back. It's important, when you introduce the saddle that you allow your horse to feel the sensation that the saddle causes in all three paces, forwards and also backwards

Because I have asked her to do something that she is familiar with, she settles into the saddle very quickly. Horses that have never worn a saddle are generally fine until you ask them to trot, and this is when you will get a reaction. Nine out of ten horses will pass through this phase very quickly and will trot quite happily. You may see the reaction again when you ask for canter or change the rein. If you have done all the work I recommend in this book, you should find that any reaction is minimal. However, you will always get an exception to the rule. When this happens interrupt the horse if he gets too blanked out and get him to change direction – the more changes of direction you can do, the quicker he will come back to you. This is the great thing about having your horse on a rope as opposed to letting him free, as it can be difficult getting him to come back to you. Letting your horse go too right brained won't help – he needs to learn to come down off the adrenaline rush so that he can think about the saddle and what you are asking of him

Once Hermione has mastered stepping backwards, I ask her to move off on to a circle through her shoulder. Because I have done all the work in this book with her prior to this point, she will understand totally what I am asking. It will feel familiar to her and help her to relax

Hermione is now tuned into what she knows and isn't really thinking about the saddle. She is light and responsive when I ask her to turn

When I asked her to canter, there was a small reaction, but this was her first canter with a saddle on. I have talked about the importance of using repetition previously, and this is one of those times that I think it's important to play the numbers game

The first bridle

The bridle often gets forgotten as we are so worried about introducing the saddle, but remember that every stage is important to your youngster.

Before moving on to this section you will need to have read 'Preparing for a bridle' (pages 108–109) to benefit from the information here.

Once you have gone through all of the preparation of putting your finger in the mouth and rubbing your hand over the eye and ears, the bridle really isn't an issue as you have already set up the cues for the horse. It's when you don't do this that you will get problems. When bridling for the first time, I always take off the noseband as you don't need it and it just gets in the way.

Taking the bridle off is equally important. It will cause you all sorts of problems if you let the bit just drop out of your horse's mouth. Take the bridle off gently, if you have problems with your horse raising his head, then you haven't put enough halter work in. All my youngsters will keep their heads low when I take the bridle off.

HOW TO ... INTRODUCE THE FIRST BRIDLE

Remember to take off the nose band

Now you can see the relationship between the exercises for preparing for a bridle – thumb in the mouth

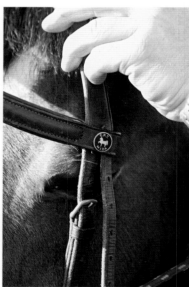

Do you remember me brushing my hand over the eye? Here our youngster calmly closes her eye as the leather passes over

Unfortunately, this youngster doesn't really understand what the bit is for, which is why her mouth is wide open. But it won't take long to teach her, and the best way is from the ground

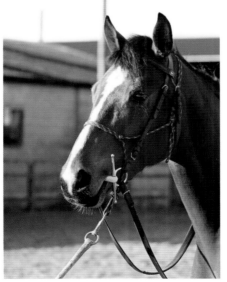

Pushing the bridle over the ear ties in with me doing the same thing with my hand

Ta-da! Bridle on. No fuss. All because we put in our groundwork and preparation

Moss understands what the bit is for as I have spent time with her on the ground. She is soft and accepting – you can't ask more from a newly backed youngster

Accepting the bit

Teaching your youngster to accept the bit is one of the main elements to getting your horse backed and ridden away, because without that acceptance you will have problems of varying degrees throughout your horse's ridden life.

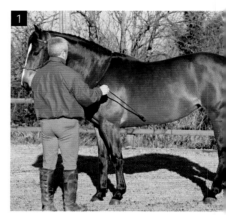

Getting any horse to accept the bit is what will allow you to communicate what you want them to do when ridden. Therefore getting that acceptance has to be a priority and can't be left out or done at a later date.

Here is a list of what a bit can teach your horse:

- To listen to your requests
- To move left or right
- To move backwards (submission)
- Flexion (vertical and laterally)
- To be respectful
- To relax the jaw, poll and neck

And the by-product of all these are:

- Lowering their head (calming down)
- Slowing down (downward transitions)
- Physical and emotional control
- Collection
- Balance
- Suppleness
- Self-carriage

I find that many people don't really understand what the bit is about and think that putting a bit in the horse's mouth prior to backing is all that is needed. We don't want the horse to only mouth the bit, we need him to understand it. A bit is a human invention, and we therefore need to teach the horse what its job is. Most resistances that arise through bitting are generally from a lack of understanding from the horse rather than the bit itself.

We need to start to ask questions with the bit so that the horse can work out the answers.

Twenty minutes a day for 10 days will educate your horse about the bit and what it is asking, for the rest of his life. I think this is a great trade off for the time invested. In this day and age of busy lives and pressurized jobs we have to become time efficient, which will have a knock-on effect with everything you do with your horse.

When I am out and about on livery yards one of the comments I hear the most is that horses won't accept the bit and that it is really slowing down any progress in their training. I know from personal experience that having a horse that is difficult in the mouth can be a hard thing to overcome – I inherited a horse will these problems, which is why I started to use the following exercises. These exercises worked well but took a little longer with an older horse to re-train but, like everything else, I have started to use the processes I use to train problem horses to improve young unspoilt horses, with great success.

We need our horses to listen to our requests as this is one of the main ways you will have of communicating with your horse from the saddle. The great thing is that these exercises can be started a long time before you back your horse and work from the ground. Then when you do eventually back your youngster you will have so

much already in place and your line of communication will already be created.

I start this exercise with my youngsters when they are anything from two upwards – you will know when your youngster is ready. You should also make sure that all your in-hand work and leading is good before starting this work.

I like to use a short stick/crop and to have the youngster bridled. The crop is not to beat my horse with but to use in the position of my leg as if I were riding. To make it easier for my youngster, I use a fence line to work along.

1 Starting on the nearside, I face my youngster with the rein in my left hand and the stick in my right. Because of all the leading training my young horse will have gone through, he leads straight and is respectful of my personal space. By using the stick where my leg would go, I ask for forward movement by tapping the stick on the horse's side.

2 I walk down the fence line encouraging my horse with the stick and quietly asking him to flex towards me as he walks on. This is to get the horse flexing and giving to me so I am not asking for a lot of flexion at first. I am looking for the horse to lower his head and relax.

3 When you have successfully achieved good flexion on one rein move on to the other. Remember that when you change over to the other side only 25 per cent of what you have taught the horse will transfer to that side, so don't be disappointed that the response at first isn't as good. Once I can get a nice give on both reins, I will start to ask for a bigger give by asking for more flexion whilst keeping the horse walking in a good rhythm.

I find that repeating this small but crucial exercise until both reins yield roughly the same will help to iron out the natural one-sidedness of most horses.

Always remember to allow your horse to straighten his neck as a reward for flexing to you.

4 Now that I am happy with the way my horse is giving to me in a straight line with lowering the head and flexing to the inside, I will move onto a 10 metre circle and start to show the horse how this flexion controls his shoulder and hips.

Notice how the white hind leg is coming through to engage and the rein in my hand is soft and loose.

5 In this picture you can see how the shoulders are moved and controlled with the soft rein. Again, once the horse has responded like this, you must allow him to straighten his neck and walk on without any flexion as a reward. This exercise is the start of the basic ask of moving from the leg to your hands and supples your young horse ready for the rider when that time comes.

Long-lining

I often get asked why I long-line young horses on a circle rather than using the lunge. My answer is that it is more like riding from the ground and actually relates to what is going to be asked of them once I am in the saddle. It teaches them to accept the bit, turn, stop, and move up and down the transitions. It also teaches them balance and to move with their hocks underneath them.

Horses that have been backed without being long-lined on a circle are more likely to be resistant to the bit, unbalanced and not understand moving away, stopping and reining back.

When I ask a youngster to do any of these, I will use an audible cue such clicking with my tongue or a kissing noise. Once I am riding, when I ask the for the same movement with my legs, seat, or hands, I can use the audible cue so that the horse recognizes that he is meant to do something.

Before I introduce long-lines to any horse, I make sure that they accept a line going behind them – you don't want to put long-lines on your horse for the first time and then find out he is going to object and flee into the next county. Standing on whichever side of your horse you feel comfortable, loop your 12 foot (3.6m) rope, pass it over your horse's head and feed it round his side and behind his quarters. You can start this exercise when your horse is quite young, which will be of great benefit, but if you have an older horse that you would like to introduce to long-lining, the same principles apply

Next take a feel on the rope and ask your youngster to turn away from you and follow the feel of the rope. This is difficult at first as he will want to move towards you, but he must think and move towards the feel. You may have to wait a while but each time you do it the wait will become shorter and shorter. Do this on both sides for at least 12 repetitions. I like to do more with a horse that is wary, but you can judge how much is needed for yourself

3 YEARS+

Equipment used for long-lining is the same as for ridden work. I use either a stirrup leather or horseman's string to tie the stirrups together under the belly, making sure that the stirrups cannot bang against the horse's elbows.

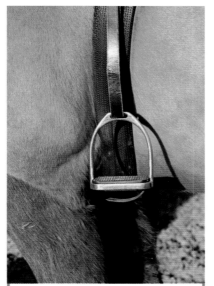

It is getting the small things wrong that spoil the bigger picture. When you are getting ready to long-line, make sure that your stirrups are set higher than your horse's elbow so that he doesn't get bashed by the stirrup iron

This stirrup iron is too low and will cause your horse discomfort whilst being long-lined and could make him reluctant to go forward

I use a simple stirrup leather to secure the stirrups whilst long-lining. I secure them quite firmly. You can also see in this picture how a longer stirrup would bang against a youngster's elbow

---

3 – THE MAGIC NUMBER

My rule of thumb when long-lining is that I change something every three circuits, whether it is the pace or direction. This keeps the horse's mind active and prevents him from switching off and becoming an automaton.

All these exercises will stand you in good stead, as when you come to ride your horse he will understand move off, slow down, stop and rein back. Not bad for a just-backed horse.

As your horse works and becomes active make sure that the throatlatch is tied up properly so that the reins don't become loose and cause and accident

Being in the correct start position is crucial to good long-lining – first, it enables you to push the outside line over your horse's quarters without him walking off and, second, it puts you in the correct position to drive your horse out onto the circle

This is the INCORRECT start position – you are too far away from your horse and you have to flick your line over his quarters causing him to walk off without you being in control

Here you can see that the outside line being flicked over his quarters has caused him to rush off – which isn't what you want

When long-lining an unbacked horse, I would take the reins off the bridle. Otherwise I leave them on and twist them into the throatlatch so that they are there ready for me for riding after the long-lining session.

Using a pair of 30 foot (9m) lines, 20 foot (6m) lunge lines are too short for the outside rein, and standing on the nearside, I put the first line over the saddle until the clip touches the floor – this allows enough line to thread through the stirrup iron up to the bit; the second line I put through the stirrup and up to the bit. Once the lines are attached, I put the rein on the offside around the horse's hindquarters.

You will need to have completed the rope exercises on page 24 before doing this and your horse must also be accustomed to something being behind him. If you missed that training, go back to that exercise *before* you long-line.

3 YEARS+

I now stand at the horse's shoulder with both reins in my hand. Using an audible cue such as clucking, I ask the horse to move off onto a circle whilst feeding the lines through my hands. I personally train my horses to noises such as clicking or clucking to keep matters simple. If you prefer to train your horse to voice commands, that is entirely up to you.

If you haven't long-lined before, to begin with you will feel awkward and uncoordinated, so keep your horse in walk until you feel more confident with the lines and have managed turning.

Turning and changing direction

Try to think about long-lining as riding from the ground and that the same principles apply – left rein takes the horse to the left and the right rein takes the horse to the right. So with your horse moving on the left rein, shorten the right rein by about 6–9 foot (1.8–2.7m). Once you have taken that amount of rein firmly without being too sharp, take a feel on that rein and this will start the change of direction. As your horse starts to change direction, let the other rein slide through your hands to allow for the turn. Because you have taken up 6–9 foot (1.8–2.7m), you should find that once the turn is made your reins are where they should be.

Now I can just imagine that you are thinking 'I will never be able to do that!' But if you can ride a horse, drive a car and ride a bicycle, you have got the dexterity needed for this. At first your circles will all look like octagons – that doesn't matter, you will get them to be round in the end.

Slowing down and speeding up

Once you have got the hang of long-lining, you can start to go up and down transitions. You will also be able to turn in trot and, when you are really good, in canter.

So how do you move up and down the gears? Whichever rein you are on it is the outside rein that influences pace and the inside rein that creates the bend. To speed up send a wave or ripple down the outside line to the horse's quarters and at the same time give an audible cue. This encourages the horse to bring his hocks underneath him, to lift his belly and to move forward. Once he is achieving what you ask, stop asking him and don't ask again until he does something different. By doing this, you will train a horse that goes for himself rather than being nagged the whole way.

When you want to slow down, take a feel on the outside rein and ask the horse to slow down. Again, once he has done as you asked, stop asking him.

Asking your horse to stop is done in the same way as slowing down except that I adjust the reins so that I get more of an even feel. I then keep a feel until the horse has stopped and allow with the reins. If he moves off again, I ask with the outside rein until he stops and keep repeating until he understands that I want him to stand.

Rein back

Once your horse is standing, you need to ask him to rein back. With a youngster, I always do this exercise at the end of a session as it does two things: one is to include backing up as a discipline; the other is to tell him that it is the end of the session and that he can rein back and relax whilst I take off all the lines.

To ask for the rein back, I move myself into a position that is more behind the horse. I again take up an even feel and maintain it until my horse takes a step back. In the early part of the training I will accept a small step back but as I progress I am looking for all four feet to move back with even steps.

Rein back is important in riding and groundwork as it helps to develop a respectful and compliant horse. At first 99 per cent of horses will resist because it is a very submissive act – initially your horse will become either very over bent or will set his neck against you. Just quietly maintain the feel until he has moved all four feet back one step. Then release the pressure and ask again

Introducing a rider

As I keep saying, you should have done all the preparation that you need to make this a completely uneventful stage in your horse's training. If you have any doubts about a successful outcome, then spend more time consolidating the foundations. I would start preparing for a rider in the following way and include it in my preparation a good few months before the actual day.

The dummy

To quickly recap, in earlier years I stated that I didn't agree with the use of a dummy rider on a young horse (yes that is a stuffed 'pretend' person). This was mainly because I had only dealt with re-backs that had gone wrong because of a dummy.

However, until very recently I did everything on my own when backing horses, and there is no doubt that a second person is useful for this process – whether they are stuffed or not!

A horse was sent to me for backing that I knew, was going to have serious issues with a rider being above his eye height. I hadn't developed the 'desensitization on the move' plan (see pages 134–135) at that stage, so I had to come up with something else. This was when I made my first dummy using old coveralls stuffed with straw, tied at the wrists and legs, and stitched at the neck. I also added clips to make attaching it easier quicker and safer.

HOW TO ... INTRODUCE THE FIRST RIDER

Before I even put the dummy on, I make sure I can chuck it about, around the horse without the youngster becoming too agitated – remember that I also now do loads of desensitization work as well

CASE HISTORY

I do not use a dummy on all horses, only those that I think might have a problem with a rider. However, I had in a lovely Arab, Clemmie, to back (used in the next section on backing) that came with a remit that because of the owner's previous illness, it was imperative that the mare was as safe as possible because it would be serious if her owner fell off. Great, I thought, an Arab that has to be bomb proof. I put on my thinking cap and contemplated the situation. Young horses are going to do a fair amount of spooking and one situation that can happen is that a youngster spooks, the rider falls down the side of the horse's neck or off to the side and this can then cause a bigger reaction. So I used the dummy to recreate this situation and trained Clemmie to cope with the dummy bobbing about, leaning right out to the side, falling forward and so on, and it worked like a dream. On her first hack she showed up me and my big horse. She was as close to bomb proof as you could get, remembering that there are no absolute guarantees with horses.

3 YEARS+

Once the horse is happy, I start by walking him around with the dummy sitting on the saddle

Now I have the perfect rider that, apart from the weight, causes all the same responses as a human rider

Other preparation exercises

1 Jump up and down at the side of them on both sides.

2 Lean into the stirrup and put weight into it.

3 Practise lifting your foot up to the stirrup. Then, to help the horse get used to somebody being higher than his eye line, try riding and leading.

Backing your youngster

The day arrives and you have left nothing to chance. Your youngster is wearing his saddle and has done lots of groundwork, all you need to do now is add a rider.

This is Clemmie, an Arab who has completed earlier work with the dummy. I have gone through everything with her that I have talked about in this book and am expecting the addition of a rider to be a total non-event.

2 Once Joey is laid over the saddle and secure, I move Clemmie's head – first to the offside and then to the nearside. This is so that Clemmie sees Joey on both sides and doesn't get a fright and shoot off. When I do move off, I ask Clemmie to move away through her shoulder, using a process that she is familiar with through circling work.

1 Before inviting Joey in to get on, I work Clemmie on the rope, with her tack on. Joey gives her a fuss and then stands facing the saddle, we have already checked that the stirrups are at the right length and that the girth is done up.

In one motion, leg your rider up and over the saddle, it is important to do this in a sweeping movement, do not wear anything that can get caught on the saddle. Notice how Joey has positioned her arm on the offside saddle flap with her left hand on the front of the saddle, this is so that if the horse does react she can push herself off and away safely.

3 Once I felt that everything was ok and had walked them both around, I asked Clemmie to go out onto the circle, again all familiar processes.

3 YEARS+

4 Going solo, it is at this point that you have to remember that Clemmie is a baby and very green. She will be quite unbalanced with the new weight of a rider and initially it will feel like riding a glass of water – formless and uncertain. When she gets like this don't treat her like a porcelain doll, she needs firm guidance and positive riding to give her confidence.

EQUIPMENT PREFERENCES

A quick note about Clemmie: you will notice that she is wearing a hackamore (a bitless bridle). This is because when I came to introduce her to a bit I noticed she had huge wolf teeth. Putting a bit in her mouth would have caused her pain and might have made her afraid of the bridle. Also, because Clemmie was sent to me for backing, I would have had to give her time off after having them removed as her mouth would be sore for at least a week.

I train horses to give to pressure so using a hackamore instead of a bitted bridle was perfect because she understood straightaway how to give to it. Her owners are actually pleased since they want to do endurance and would love to ride her bitless. They will, however, remove her wolf teeth at some point.

5 Here Clemmie has got stuck, Joey asks her with an open hand, just quietly, to move her head from side to side and it helps her to become unstuck and move on.

We ended the session with Clemmie by doing a few circuits of the school in walk and a few strides in trot. To finish Joey asked her to back up, again no problems there as it is something she knows how to do.

Riding on from day one

Now the fun begins! You have your whole future together, but the training still continues.

Day 2

I get Joey on as I did the day before, but Clemmie is going solo much quicker. This time Joey carries an over and under (whip wop) as I don't want her using more leg to get Clemmie going if she gets sticky. I always want a horse to be responsive to my legs. When Clemmie gets stuck, I want Joey to use the over and under. Joey will first ask with her legs and if there is no response, she uses the rope to go over and behind her leg, but in quite a slow rhythm. The aim is not to sting or hurt Clemmie but to stimulate her eye, causing her to move forward from the rope. When I use it, I say in my head 'get in front of the leg', this makes me use it over, back and over again, then quit. With some horses you may have to do it more than once and increase the speed of the rope, but Clemmie is sensitive and needs asking politely. She is soon going around the arena like she's been doing it all her life

Days 3, 4 and 5

Over the next few days we are going to continue in the same vein, but I will pop Joey on and go solo straight away. Clemmie's owner is going to be taking her home in two weeks, so I need to get her ready to hack out. This can be done in the arena and I am going to be repeating lots of things that I have done on the ground.

Walking over poles

Walking between drums – start with them quite far apart and bring them closer together

Standing between drums – it is important when you are out hacking to teach your horse to stand so that junctions don't become a problem

Although Clemmie is on the rope here, Joey on Sonny is riding the circle in the opposite direction so that Clemmie gets used to things coming towards her

Day 6

We worked with these exercises until the Sunday when we took Clemmie for her first hack. It just happened to be the village car boot sale so there was lots of traffic and people in the village. Although Clemmie looked, she didn't do anything that would cause any worry, she was naturally curious

WHAT NEXT?

My suggestion now for a young horse would be to hack out three or four times a week for about 20–30 minutes at a time, but I would not turn away.

Going home

After a week of this work, Clemmie's owner came to ride her and take her home. Even if I am blowing my own trumpet, Clemmie's owner was stunned that her baby had grown into such a sensible girl. But she still wanted to ride her like a baby, which left Clemmie feeling very unsure as she was used to leadership. As soon as I explained to Clemmie's owner that she must ride her as though she was a grown up horse, she felt the difference immediately and Clemmie visibly relaxed and got on with her job.

Clemmie is now at home and we received an email to say that she hasn't put a foot wrong and has hacked out on her own and in company.

On the hack we had to cross two fords that still had enough water in them to cause Clemmie to not want to go through. Getting Joey to use her over and under and using Jo (my horse) as a lead, it took about a minute to get Clemmie through. Remember my thoughts on repetitions? Well Clemmie went back and forth through the water a good dozen times at each ford and hasn't looked back since

Desensitization on the move

In addition to the desensitization work that you do from the ground (see pages 82–89), you also need to do it on the move.

Another example of a horse teaching me something comes from Trigo, my Lusitano stallion. At the time he was with a British rider but she was having real problems with him and asked if I could visit them. What I saw was a nervous and very hot little horse that couldn't stand still and if you so much as sneezed, he would have a heart attack! He did everything at a million miles an hour.

Trigo ended up coming to stay with me and he really wasn't easy. He would panic at everything, such as if my jacket rustled, and if a mucking-out fork scraped on the barrow, he would try to climb the stable door. I knew I had to come up with something that would help Trigo as it was obvious he was a lovely horse.

I started by desensitizing him from the ground, which he responded to really well. I then came up with the idea of taking that concept up into the saddle, as horses have to deal with fear from a ridden perspective.

These exercises are excellent if you have a horse that is nervous of sudden sounds or movement or that spooks at tannoys or bunting, doesn't like the dressage judge or is a nightmare out hacking. I can't stress enough though that you cannot do this without having first done your groundwork. If you do try them without that preparation, you could end up having a nasty accident.

The exercises worked a treat for Trigo and he was taken to the Iberian performance show shortly afterwards, where he was fantastic. It has worked well since with other horses, but I repeat, you must *not* do this unless your desensitization is good from the ground.

I start by carrying my lunge whip like a schooling whip and move it around the horse until he is comfortable with it, then I undo the lash of the whip and let it drag on the floor as the horse is walking about. Next I start to move it from front to back and swing it higher and higher until it is above the horse's eye. You need to repeat this on both sides. You are looking for regularity in paces and head carriage.

Next I move the whip over his head from side to side with the lash passing in front of his face. Notice that this horse is giving me his undivided attention – this is still all new to him and he wants to keep an eye on me. Once he feels more comfortable, he will split his attention between me and his surroundings.

When you want to change the rhythm or pattern of the way you swing the lash, always go back to halt to show this change to your horse. When he is comfortable, then move up to walk.

We are now on the move with the whip moving from side to side – notice how he is now splitting his attention.

His attention is still split, even though I am whirling the whip around his head like a helicopter.

Here we have a nice square halt, a calm horse on a relaxed rein. The whip is being cracked here quite loudly and he is being such a star.

Riding on from day one

Right from the start, Echo (Balinmore Irish Rebel, 16.2½hh purebred Irish Draught) was different, not the least because he was ten months old when normally we have weanling foals. Even then he was special in many ways and had a magnetic personality.

The day that we went to see him he was being incredibly difficult. Echo set his neck and dragged my husband past me and shot back to the gate.

We almost didn't buy him, but someone was looking out for us that day. Something startled him and he stopped dead and arched his neck. In that instance I got goosebumps and I saw 'Superstar' written all over him.

When he came home he was unruly. He tried it on with everyone. Outside he was selectively deaf and thought barging and being generally obnoxious was acceptable behaviour. First he tried to pick on my gelding, Magellan, who had other ideas and set him straight immediately. He thought we were a far safer bet and outside he would try to bully us instead – barging, charging off and rearing if he didn't want to do something.

It was odd because there really wasn't a nasty bone in his body and he was marvellous with our son. In the stable he was angelic, but outside he was downright naughty. I knew if I could get through to him he would be a lovable gentle giant. I managed to sort these problems out, but then two more came along which I couldn't solve.

I arranged to have him gelded but instinct said there was definitely 'something' about him. Again, someone, somewhere intervened. On the day of his operation the heavens opened, a small lake appeared in the field and the vet cancelled.

I decided to show him and his first outing was to the Royal Show. He won his class but I found when leading him I couldn't stop him from crashing into me. He wouldn't respect my personal space and I nearly ended up being flattened by him.

We went to several more shows and he was made champion and supreme at them all. He won male youngstock champion and reserve supreme youngstock champion – as a yearling! Through them all it was a nightmare as he crashed into me constantly.

Then the nipping started. I half expected it, being a colt, but it was awful and I tried everything I knew to stop both problems, but nothing worked.

I didn't want a fight or to frighten him, but the behaviour wasn't safe and I had to do something. It wasn't nastiness, just seriously coltish behaviour that needed checking.

Things went downhill when one day he nipped me really hard. He gave me a look of 'Oops! Sorry! … But this is *really fun* … let's do it again … harder!' I'm sure you know the sort of nip I mean – skin right on the end of the teeth, twist and pull! He knew full well it was wrong and he was off like lightning. But he was so quick and got you before you knew it.

Despair and tears arrived along with the alarmingly huge and painful purple bruise on my arm. I realized I needed help fast and set out to find it before someone really got hurt – namely me!

I had heard about Max and looked at his website. It was evident that here was someone who taught both horse and owner – not just one or the other. Max came to see Echo in March 2006 and contacting him was one of the best decisions I have ever made.

Typically, it rained buckets the day before Max came, so short of attaching water-skis we couldn't work outside. First, we concentrated on Echo's nipping and in ten seconds Max showed us how to stop him. I'll never forget the look of surprise on Echo's face – which mirrored my own. A simple solution, simply applied, but highly effective. After only two days of using the technique, Echo stopped nipping.

Max spent several hours with us and I learned more in that short time than I have done in many years. He is a quiet, unassuming gentleman with a great empathy for horses – and with the much needed patience and a sense of humour for owners.

Echo's problems turned out to be fairly easy to stop. Max easily showed me how by giving me clear and concise instructions, without talking down to me (which I hate) and making it fun too!

I learned an invaluable lesson that day – you can train with kindness (as I always try to do) but you are entitled to defend yourself when necessary and respect can be gained without causing conflict and mistrust on both sides.

Max taught us groundwork and the use of his halter and rope. This equipment is easy and effective to use when you know how and I wouldn't be without it now. Max even made me a leather version of the halter that I can use at shows.

In the weeks after our training session, I followed Max's instructions to the letter. There really is no point taking his advice and then giving it a half-hearted attempt. You've got to *want* to make a change and be prepared to work for it.

I continued using groundwork and Echo improved daily, quickly learning to walk his own line, shoulder to shoulder with me, without bumping into me, tripping me up or generally running me down.

Max's tuition proved so successful that in June 2006 I decided to be brave and took Echo to the East of England two-year-old's loose jumping classes. He was calm, gentle and well-behaved. With no problems at all we finished in the top line-up. For some reason he was visited by loads of children who fell in love with him.

He's literally gone from strength to strength. He has an amazing jump (being from a line of international Grade As) and is immensely powerful for a young horse. He's turned into a true Irish Draught – kind, intelligent, accepting, loves children (but can't eat a whole one!), bold but sensible, ` occasionally a bit stupid but always loyal.

On a cold day in February of 2007 I thought my heart would burst with pride. Just short of a year from when Max came to see us and at only three years old, Echo passed the tough Irish Draught stallion inspection to become 'Balinmore Irish Rebel – Grade 1 Stallion'. His fabulous temperament, manners and trainability caused much comment and I told people about Max and what he had done for us.

I was honoured that I could stand next to this majestic and kind stallion and call him my friend.

Thanks to Max, Echo is a long, long way from when he first came home. His future is hopefully now very bright as he starts his stud training for AI and then goes to a professional showjumper with his impeccable manners and star burning more brightly than I ever dared hope.

Mandi Meer

Case study: Spirit

Dominant, intelligent, anglo-arab, chestnut, mare – say's it all really doesn't it! Well, that is Spirit. I have owned Spirit since she was weaned and she has always been a challenge – spirit by name and spirit by nature.

I originally called Max because Spirit had stopped loading. At the anglo-arab national championships at Keysoe, I spent four hours trying to get her into the lorry with her behaviour ranging from planting her feet to rearing up and going over sideways. It really was a miracle that she didn't seriously injure herself or anyone else! I vowed from that day that I would never go through that again!

When I introduced Max to Spirit, she immediately snarled at him to see if she could intimidate him like she does so many other people. Max just ignored her and proceeded to check her out physically to rule out any pain issues that may be causing her behaviour. She was quite tight in her shoulders and a little behind the poll, which was most probably as a result of her antics when loading and her other various misbehaviours.

Max took her into the menage and used the halter to teach her about pressure and release, allowing her to make her own mistakes and judgements and to decide what would be the best course of action in her own mind. She is a very intelligent mare and after throwing her tantrums at Max, she quickly realized that she wasn't going to intimidate or bully him and he was in fact the one moving *her* around to his requests instead of vice versa.

Max showed me, how to use the halter and line, and where to position myself – it was all very different to what I'd been used to!

Max then took Spirit to the lorry – where she threw a few more tantrums, and destroyed a few slats on the ramp! The thinking time that Max allowed was crucial to Spirit as she *will not* be bullied into anything, so it really did have to be of her own free will. After about 25 minutes Spirit was loading nicely. Max gave me a programme to work from and we loaded 20 times a day for ten days, by which point she was loading herself!

An odd thing happened during those days after Max had been out. Spirit has always been a 'my way or the highway' kind of girl – fidgety, mardy, won't stand still, won't be tied up quietly and so on. But following Max's visit her whole attitude changed – the groundlines had been redrawn and I was in charge again (even though I hadn't actually realized she didn't think I was in charge before!). I now had a horse that actually had a few seconds of thinking time before she reacted, a little more patience and more co-operation. Everyone on the yard started commenting how she seemed much quieter and less stressed. She was happier in her own skin.

I kept in touch with Max as Spirit would never be a walk in the park. She would be three in the September and I would need another 'plan' for her backing. I continued with the groundwork and we had lots more good days than bad – Spirit always needed the point underlining but as the months went by she became better in every way.

By July I had put a saddle on Spirit with girth up and stirrups down without her even fluttering an eyelash. I took her to a demo day in the August with the intention of getting on her.

At the demo, Max asked me what we'd been doing and I explained about the saddle and how we'd been for walks in it and how she was *so* good! Well obviously she would make a liar of me. Max tacked her up and sent her off on the 12 foot rope and she exploded like an all-American rodeo horse! She did the whole nine yards and I was bright red with embarrassment. Needless to say, Spirit had decided she wasn't quite ready for the whole 'on board' thing.

Max showed me how to desensitize her to the saddle at movement and introduced us both to long-lining. He then sent us away with a plan for the saddle and accepting having things above her. Spirit never takes anything on face value – everything has to be justified and explained. We went away with our plan and did just as we'd been told and once again Spirit trusted what she'd been shown through the ground exercises.

By October everything just felt right and I got on board my beautiful, intelligent, challenging mare. Within two weeks we were hacking out in company. Spirit just loves work and seems to relish having a job in life. We kept up with the long-lining to encourage balance and fitness. In addition she does ride and lead off my other horse and is excellent in traffic. I couldn't have asked for more.

The main lesson I learned from Max about Spirit is that she will always need the groundwork to underline her place and role. During the last six months she has done just as Max said she would in that she has moved up the pecking order in the field. Now this may not seem

very important, but with that change also came a change in her behaviour. Spirit slipped back into her old ways of being bolshy and rude, not respecting my personal space as much and making her feelings well and truly known in her ridden work. The changes were subtle over a couple of months and I didn't realize what had happened until she threw a big strop and reared under saddle when she couldn't get her own way.

I took a long hard look at what had happened, stepped back and thought about things. I had a chat with Max and it all fell into place like a neat jigsaw. Spirit had moved up in the field over my gelding and was trying to move up over me!

It was back to the groundwork, which I had been shamefully neglecting as I'd been enjoying hacking her so much. The change in her behaviour within two sessions was astonishing – the manners and patience came back and she calmed immediately as she realized the rules were still in place.

So I suppose the groundwork for Spirit is a bit like a diet for the 'metabolically disadvantaged' – a life change that will have to be continued and not be just a quick fix.

The whole change in her attitude since that first day with Max is overwhelming. She will always be questioning and quick but she values the rules that Max gave her and is happier knowing her position in the world is not at the top, as that's a lonely place to be when you are still young and learning. Both Spirit and I will be forever grateful that her intelligence could be harnessed by Max and that she did not end up being known as vicious, ill-tempered and dangerous, but will have a good, useful life as a quality riding horse!

Thanks again Max, we really appreciate it!

Susie and Spirit

Max's comment: I don't think that your neglect of the groundwork over hacking her out was a bad thing as young horses need to go and see the world at large, but it is nice to know that the groundwork is there to get your relationship back on line.

Case study: Moss

Moss is a 3-year-old, 16hh Irish Sport Horse that I purchased in August 2007 after a long search for a nice youngster to bring on. She was halter broken, had worn a bit and done a bit of lungeing, but she was pretty much a blank canvas. She was nicely put together and had that little something about her that made me say 'yes!' there and then.

From day one she showed me that she was a very quick learner. I did a week or so on groundwork and getting her to understand personal space a bit more, keeping her listening to me instead of getting distracted, and explaining to her that I AM here to be listened to! Then we went off to a local show.

We didn't come last as such, we came third … but there were only three in the class! It was a big question to ask so soon – she was very giddy, throwing herself about with her tail up, not like her at all! But it was good experience and made me realize she needed lots more work, especially on learning what the bit is there for. I'd mostly done everything off a horseman's halter before that and it was like she was saying, 'Look, I know you want me to listen to you, but there's ALL this other stuff going on, and LOOK, I've got this THING in my MOUTH!' She looked gorgeous though, and it was the first little window of her proving to me that she could show off when she needed to – she certainly rose to the occasion!

So, back to more groundwork and long-lining, de-spooking work with tarpaulin (she can now step on, follow, and have tarpaulin draped over her head!) tractors (they're ok until they move position – how come nobody told her they were going to be moved?!), and loading work so we could go up to the indoor school for a play. All of this went really well.

Then we went to a clinic with Max (an 80 mile round trip and she loaded and travelled like a pro!). I went with the intention of asking for an assessment of our groundwork so far and some hints and tips on where to go next with her training. Lo and behold the 'where to go next' bit ended up with her being backed. I was so proud of her! She behaved like an absolute star!

I took her home and did some more long-lining and halter work and then I jumped on her myself a few times. It went reasonably well, although I did have one session where she tried to roll and then had a buck, which was fine, but made me think, 'Do you know what, I want to make sure this gets done properly.' I didn't want to get myself in a mess with her and then have to send her away to sort it out. I wanted her first ridden experiences to be the very best they could be right from the start, and Max was obviously the best person to do that! That meant another trip southwards. She travelled brilliantly and calmly walked into her stable and started to munch her hay.

Moss's visit was going to be over the Christmas period and I knew I would really miss her, but I received phone calls from Max and lots of photos so that I could see how she was progressing. All in all, her stay was four weeks. Because I lived so far away it wasn't possible to visit during that period, but when I went to pick her up, Max had me do everything from tacking her up myself to riding in the arena and then out on a hack. I got back a horse that could hack out in company or on her own; she was so independent and relaxed. I think it is always a worry when you send your youngster away that you are not going to get the same horse back.

Max and Joey (Max's rider) also did some loose jumping with Moss, which showed me that she could get off the ground, and Joey had popped her over a very small cross country fence out on a hack. Although I won't do that myself for a little while, at least I have the knowledge that I can if I want to and that Moss wasn't even slightly worried about it.

Sal and Moss

Max's comment: Moss arrived and, as her owner said, I had already worked with the youngster and knew what she was all about. She is a nice mare but one that, if you let her, could have the potential to quietly dominate the relationship. Sticking to the groundwork and getting her to use her brain will be key to keeping Moss on the straight and narrow.

This was a good case study as Sal, Moss's owner, had put into place the basic principles that I suggest all young horses should do, so now I could prove that it really does help with the next stage of Sal and Moss's life together. There were several things that showed me that although Moss had worn a bit and had been long-lined, she still didn't realize what the bit was for. This backed up my theory that you need to train your youngster to understand what the job of a bit is (see Teaching your youngster to accept the bit pages 122–123).

Second, and on a much more positive note, was that all the desensitizing training that Sal had done stood Moss in good stead as she was great to hack out; nothing phased her, a pheasant could fly up or a hare run from under her feet and you could see her thinking 'that old nugget again', but at the same time she was a nice lively ride, in a manageable way, which is what we are all after. Also while she was with us, Moss was very woolly and getting sweaty in her work, so I decided that a trace clip would help her. Again because of the work Sal had done with her, she stood like a pro in the wash down area to be clipped.

Sal did well to put enough work into Moss to make the backing process so much easier and it was just another day in the life of Moss.

We wish Sal and Moss all the best for their bright future together.

Questions and answers

Q I have now backed my youngster but I am struggling to get her to go off the leg and feel as though I am having to get too strong with my legs at this early stage.

A You are right, you definitely don't want to start your ridden life using such a strong leg. The ideal situation would have been to use an audible cue such as clucking or a kissing noise whilst working with your horse on the ground doing your circling work, long-lining or any work that involved moving the feet. Doing this means your horse is cued that a cluck or a kissing noise means move your feet. It is not too late to implement this but you will have to go right back to the beginning.

However, the easiest thing for you now is to use what is known as an over and under or whip wop. This is used in a motion similar to the way cowboys use their long split reins. It creates a visual stimulus behind the eye causing the horse to move forward. Use a neck strap whilst doing this exercise.

Have your whip wop ready and use it from the nearside to the offside and back again. If you are struggling with this visually, then think about the cowboys leaving town. First, sit quietly and ask your horse to move off with the lightest pressure from your leg. If she doesn't respond, then use your whip wop, you will find that she will shoot forward, which is why you need a neck strap. Don't do anything now until she slows down or you have asked her to stop. Repeat the exercise until she moves off with the lightest pressure from your leg and you don't have to use your whip wop. This encourages forward movement, and will also teach your horse to do what is asked until you ask for something different. It stops all the nagging and arguing.

When I start hacking out my youngsters, I always carry a whip wop in case I come against a scenario where I need to coax them through or past something.

Clemmie had started to get a little stuck, so I asked Joey to use the whip wop, which is made from a bit of old rope folded in half, with a knot tied to form a loop so it can then sit around your wrist when you don't need it

Q My youngster is terrified of anything coming towards her or up behind her when we are out hacking. What can I do to help her?

A Although you would have to be very careful as horses on roads with cars are a recipe for disaster, there is a lot you can do at home to prepare you and your horse for these situations.

First, I would make sure I had thoroughly gone through all the desensitization exercises in this book. Until my horse was perfect at home, I wouldn't even consider going on the roads – if it wasn't perfect, it would be like driving a car that had no steering and brakes.

Second, I would rope in a friend and their horse and start to do some exercises in the school. Get your friend to ride up behind you and past, and then do the same in the other direction. Start by standing your horse on the fence line – she will flinch and be quite worried by it but she will get through that. Once she is happy to stand and let them ride past in both directions, increase your pace to walk and when she is happy, move to trot and canter.

When you first start, ask your friend to ride past leaving quite a bit of space between them and you, but as your horse becomes more confident, reduce the space until your knees are almost touching.

If your horse struggles with this, go back to the beginning and ask your friend to stand off the outside track and ride past her in both directions, narrowing the space as you go.

Once she is coping with all of this, you can ask some more friends to join you in the arena. This is also a great exercise for horses that don't like crowded collecting rings at shows.

Q I am currently backing my youngster but he is very nervous of me when I go to get on. I don't want to get on and fall off in case I panic him. Have you got any suggestions?

A It is in these situations that I would now use a dummy. I make this by using an A-frame made of blue plastic tubing. I then use a pair of overalls and stitch up the feet and arms and add clips to both arms and legs to make it easier to attach to the horse. I stuff the legs and arms with straw put in my A-frame and tie up the neck.

Please don't think that you can just chuck this straight up on your horse. You will need to go through some desensitization exercises with him so that he becomes very blasé about your new rider. Once he is ok with this, you can pop him on and just walk around holding the dummy on. When you feel it is ok, attach the dummy to the saddle like a real rider. Clip each foot to a stirrup, and I also put a leather strap on the front of the saddle allowing me to attach the arms. I then do everything from groundwork to long-lining with my new rider for at least a week and sometimes two.

The dummy will help your horse to get used to something bobbing about high up behind his eye line, which is what makes many horses nervous. If your dummy does fall forward, this is also a good exercise as when a rider comes off it is generally down the side of the horse's neck.

Q I have a rising 4 year old that I would like to introduce to the road ready for when he is started. What is the best and safest way to do this?

I thought about long-lining him out but someone said I should walk him out in hand next to his side to get him used to it.

A In this day and age roads are such dangerous places, unless you are lucky enough to live in a situation where there is no traffic. I wouldn't take a young horse out on lines or otherwise to 'get used to' traffic. What if, while you were on one of these outings, and you and your horse got such a scare that it affected you both forever?

What I would do though is a lot of preparation so that when I do take my youngster out on the road, they are in a position to deal with any scary thing that comes their way.

See the section on desensitization (pages 82–89) and work a lot with things like the bag on a stick and the work with the training stick and string.

Also, when you are working on a circle from the ground, get a friend to ride their horse on the outer circle but in the opposite direction as this will get your youngster used to objects coming towards him.

Make sure all your lateral work on the ground is good so that if your horse sees something spooky in the hedge you are able to control his shoulders and quarters so that you can get him past without looking at the object.

Make it fun and use your imagination. In the school, use things such as bollards, fill up black sacks with straw and place them randomly in the school – try to think of possible hazards and re-create the situations you may come across on a hack.

Do not even attempt to go on the roads until your horse does all these things without batting an eyelid.

Q I long-line my youngster on a circle but was wondering if it has to be done on a circle, or whether I can introduce any other exercises. I sometimes feel that my horse is getting bored.

A Once you are established on a circle there is no reason why you can't add loads of variety to your long-lining. Think of all the things you do when riding in the school and do the same lines – serpentines, changing direction at said markers, lateral work, figure of eights and the list goes on. However, it will mostly have to be done in walk unless you are incredibly fit.

Only attempt these movements if you have good control in place. If you don't, you will get yourself into trouble with your horse being so far in front of you – if he decides to take off, then there's not a lot you can do about it, which is why I don't long-line out on the roads.

To successfully achieve the above, you need to be able to turn your horse as and when you want as this will disengage him so that he will be unable to get away from you.

Remember the rule of thumb when long-lining is to change something after every three circuits, whether it is pace or direction. By doing this your horse won't get bored as it will keep his brain active by giving him something to think about.

3 YEARS+

Q The youngster I have bred to do dressage with eventually is turned out 24/7 at the moment, so I haven't really had to handle him a lot. How important is it that I teach him to back up when all I want to be able to do is lead him in a straight line? He won't be living in a stable until he is about three and then it will only be in the evenings.

A You may only want to lead him in a straight line at the moment but eventually you'll need him to back up, even if it is to move out of your way in a gateway. Why leave this exercise until your youngster is so big and strong that he will object?

Backing up for an older horse, especially one that is dominant or already thinks he is top of the pecking order, is hard and can cause a few problems, whereas if you teach him when he is young, he won't think to question it.

For me, backing up is a key task and the reason I see it as such is that once it is in place it will have a profound effect on everything else you do with your horse. It will give you respect in the stable as it teaches the horse to move out of your way when you enter with a haynet or feed. Getting your youngster to move back when you enter his space reinforces to him that you are the leader of your small herd. This will also transfer to the field gateway.

Later in life, backing up will go towards discipline, collection, submission and giving you better brakes when needed in times of fright or over excitement.

I feel it is a must-have discipline so that I can have a relaxed and calm horse in all situations. When I first meet a horse, I ask him to back up. His reaction to this question will tell me a huge amount about him – whether he is well trained and has just reached a small difficulty or whether he thinks he is the boss in his relationship with his owner.

Horses that object to being backed up are the ones that normally quietly dominate the relationship and have their owner dance to their tune. Quite often it is done in such a passive way that the owners don't even realize that they are at their horses' beck and call. The response on the face many owners is quite funny, because the penny suddenly drops and they know it is true. By changing these small elements you will change the whole dynamic of your relationship.

Backing up is key to many of the tasks you do with your horse, from going through gates to loading and unloading. Having a youngster that backs up willingly will make every-day life with your horse much easier

Conclusion

There are probably going to be a few people reading this book that think, 'well I didn't do anything with my youngster and he turned out fine', and that is probably very true.

However, I also come across a lot of people on my travels who are at the end of their tether because it isn't going well, and what was supposed to be their dream has turned into a complete nightmare.

It's a long time from a foal being born to it being old enough to back, so rather than let it go pear-shaped, why not get yourself a plan of action over that period for you to put in enough work to make owning a youngster that dream?

Regardless of what you ultimately want to do with your youngster, whether it is to hack around the lanes or compete at local or affiliated level, the most important factor is that you and your horse are safe. Don't get yourself into a situation where you daren't come out of the school because your horse can't behave safely on the roads.

Don't become one of those horse owners who can't control their horse and when he plays up and spooks at something his behaviour becomes something or someone else's fault. If your horse cannot be lead past any situation without messing about, the only person who can be blamed is you, for not establishing the ground rules and respect.

Finally, one of the biggest thrills for me is to see the look on the face of someone who has waited all that time to finally see their horse backed and then ridden away.

I know for me, I still love to hear how the youngsters I bred are getting on and it is my intention this year to put my mare in foal, and this time I am going to breed a show jumper. The mum, Vogue, by Orame, is still young and hasn't done too much in her life, but she is so amazingly bred that I would like to put her to Arko, and who knows? I might just breed myself a superstar.

Enjoy your youngsters, stay safe and let me know how you get on by joining our online community at www.richard-maxwell.com.

Suggested reading

For a more detailed step-by-step of circling work and long-lining, I would recommend reading *Unlock Your Horse's Talent* by Richard Maxwell and Johanna Sharples (David & Charles, 2007).

For more lateral work from the ground that you could do with your horse once he can carry a saddle, I would recommend reading my *Maximize Your Horsemanship* (David & Charles, 2006).

A good book to read if you are looking to improve yourself in the saddle is *Enlightened Equitation* by Heather Moffett (David & Charles, 2002).

For a more visual effect you can check out my DVDs at www.richard-maxwell.com in the merchandise section. For all equipment also check out www.richard-maxwell.com.

Acknowledgments

I would like to thank all of the following people as they have played a huge part in my knowledge to date and to those who are part of my ongoing journey.

Major Cole, York Riding School – Major Cole inspired me as a youngster to be a great horseman.

Dougie MacGregor (ex-riding master of the Household Cavalry) – Dougie was the first person who believed in me and encouraged me to strive for better results.

Terry Pendry, oops, Sir Terry Pendry – if it wasn't for Terry I would never have met Monty Roberts and I definitely wouldn't be where I am now.

Monty Roberts – for very obvious reasons. I hope one day he will be proud of me and what I have achieved, no matter what. If it hadn't been for Monty, I wouldn't have even known there was a different way to work with horses.

Pat Parelli – without him even knowing, his principles also influenced the way I work now.

Andy Andrews (RIP) – for me the greatest horseman that ever lived, maybe not in the sense of Monty or Pat but what he didn't know about horses and their ailments or leg problems wasn't worth knowing. He always had a potion, a story and the time for fourteen cups of tea even if clients were waiting. Andy I miss you as a friend and a mentor and I thank you for everything you taught me.

Sam, my wife. Who has written this book and *Maximize Your Horsemanship*. I forgot to thank Sam in the last book, sorry hun! Sam is my rock, my biggest supporter and critic. Although it is me that you see in all the photos and demos, we are very much a team. After 23 years together no one knows me better.

My boys, James, William and Jack. Everyday they bring a smile to my face. It's so exciting for me now that they are showing an interest. I have definitely found my next pupil in William. James is interested in the breeding side of horses and Jack is determined, even at the age of 7, to be a farrier. However, at 7, I wanted to be a fireman!

Thank you to Jo Legh-Smith (nee Sharples) for rescuing us when we got stuck and putting the book into a user-friendly format. Jo has been expecting during both *Maximize Your Horsemanship* and this book. I promise, Jo, I won't write any more books at such inconvenient times.

Thanks to Nikki Collard. Nikki runs my life and my diary and always goes above and beyond when it comes to her time. You can contact Nikki on +44 (0) 1440 702327 or by email on equestservices@btinternet.com if you would like any further information on consultations, clinics or having your youngster backed. www.richard-maxwell.com

Thanks to Jane Trollope from David & Charles who always stays calm when Sam calls having a panic about writing the book and has been a great supporter.

I would also like to thank Heather Moffett of Enlightened Equitation who is now working with me to improve my seat and to further my knowledge in classical riding. It has been a long time since I have done anything for myself and has really enthused me and got me out of a rut of doing the same old same old.

John Lyons – with whom I have spent a week on a course. I haven't felt so excited about the future since I first met Monty Roberts.

Just to finish off, I owe a huge thank you to Karen Simpson who gave me Trigo. We are going to start some jumping with him soon and then do some intro events and train towards working equitation. I look forward to an exciting future for us both.

Thank you to you for buying this book and for supporting all that I do and all that I will do in the future.

Index

Horses' names are shown in italic. Page numbers in italic indicate illustrations.